my Joe

by Shahe Nahler

Shahe Nahler

Sing to
the Lord with
thankful hearts.
~Colossians 3:16

Table of Contents

Acknowledgements

I know it sounds cheesy to say that I have loved my journey with the Lord, but I do. I wouldn't change and I don't regret a thing because to do so would be to change or regret what He has done and changed in me.

I know it sounds cheesy to say that I love my Jesus, but I do and I always will. I cannot imagine my heart without Him.

I know it sounds cheesy to say that I love my Joe, but I do, whole-heartedly. I cannot imagine life without him.

I love my Aalia and my Adam too. They are the very best brown babies a mama could ever ask for or to be loved by!

God is good! – Shahe Nahler

Preface

I was born in 1967 in Kabul, Afghanistan.

I have an Afghan father and an American mother.

I have a "citizen born abroad" birth certificate.

I was born with dual citizenship.

I have been married and divorced.

I am a mother to a daughter and a son.

I was spiritually born again in 1995.

I have a Heavenly Father and an eternal home.

I have a Savior; His name is Jesus.

I have a testimony of leaving Islam, becoming a Christian, and living a new life in Jesus.

I have a story of letting go of Islam, living as a Christian, and loving my Jewish Jesus.

This is my story of loving God, falling in love with Jesus, and marrying my Joe.

Introduction

The only thing harder than writing a book is starting that book. How do you start writing? I have spent most of this year introducing you to myself through book one and book two. Now I find myself wondering how to introduce you to the part of me that is the newest. I thought this was going to be the "easy" book because it is the freshest part to remember, but in some ways, it seems harder.

So, I find myself on my front porch in my rocking chair. I rock and pray. I pray and rock.

Lord help me to do this again. Help me to put into words what You have done in me. Help me to honor You in all that I do. In Jesus' Name, I pray, Amen.

The rocking of the chair comforts me. I look out in my front yard and see green grass and lots of trees. I would love to say pretty flowers, but the deer have eaten them. It is a hot day. Very hot. The trees are numerous, and the sunshine pops through in patches of glorious light as if highlighting this area or that. The shade trees have beckoned the deer to come in closer.

Last year we watched the mama deer raise her triplets. We have spent many a day watching them play and grow. We named them Hailey, Logan, and Landon after a special set of siblings we know and love. We also named the mama deer Miss Tammy and the seven-point buck Mr. Bob. For over a year, we have watched and fed this deer family. We love this deer family.

We love another dear family. Mr. Bob and Miss Tammy are married, and they have three children: Hailey, Logan, and Landon. As far back as I can remember, since walking through the doors of the church, Mr. Bob and Miss Tammy were there. They had loved on my kids and me before they had kids of their own. As my children grew, so did their family.

Hailey was born first. Miss Tammy had worked for Mr. Richard before I did. When she left to stay home with Hailey, I replaced her at the church. Usually, when one person replaces another person at work, it can produce an awkward situation. But I never felt anything awkward about how Tammy and I approached each other. She loved on me beyond just being a good person, but in a way Christ, Himself would have. She always helped and guided and grew me up into that position. She became more than a source of how to do work-related tasks. She became a real friend.

Hailey was born when I started working at the church. Logan was born when I went to work at the second church. And Landon was born as I returned to work at my home church. I still look back with great fondness at how my work career can be defined by their babies.

Now our families are growing up. Their kids and my kids have always loved on and played with each other despite the age gap. This dear family, and I guess I would have to include Mr. Richard, are constants in my life. They are loving, generous, helpful, and fun to be with. They are Christ-like.

I always wondered how someone would fit into my life if I were ever to remarry. I spent most of my singleness spinning around in circles shouting "la la la la" or "when pigs fly" at the very mention of marriage. I always figured that if God were to introduce someone into my life, He would have to set him directly in front of me, slap me upside the head, and proceed to tell me that this guy is the one for me. I also figured that, when I introduced this new guy to Mr. Bob, Miss Tammy, Hailey, Logan, Landon, and Mr. Richard, if they did not like him or if he did not fit in well, it would be the door for him!

But now sitting on this porch, I see my deer triplets. They have grown. When they were little, we called them Hailey, Logan, and Landon without knowing if they were boys or girls. We had no idea. But they have grown up. Really, grown up. The triplets grew up to be one girl and two boys. Perfect!

Hailey is petite and pretty and loved by her brothers. This applies to both our dear Hailey and our deer Hailey. Logan and Landon have started growing their antlers. They are strong and tall. There is an air of majesty about them. Regal with strong necks and muscles. They are alert and walk with strength and grace. That goes for Logan and Landon too. Both love the Lord and are learning to walk in His strength and with His grace.

God is good to give us dear families and deer families. It is good to have constants in life especially if they are Christ-like.

God is also good to introduce new people who fit into our lives and fit into His plan for our lives. My prayer is that, as you read this book, you get introduced to my husband Jesus and my husband, Joe. One husband is perfect, and one is not, but both are very important to me. Both are very dear to me. Both walk with strength and grace because both walk in the ways of the Lord of the Universe Who created them.

So join me on my porch. Pull up a rocking chair, and I will tell you about my journey, my Jesus, and my Joe. We can sit a while and have some lemonade. Joe makes great lemonade! We can watch the deer graze in the grass and eat my flowers. We can watch the hummingbirds eat from our feeder and partake in aerial combat maneuvers as they fight one another off guarding that very feeder. They make a buzzing noise as they fly past you. When they come into close contact with one another, they speak a funny language that sounds like squeaky toys. Who knew? So let's get to rocking and sipping and squeaking. God is good!

Ruth

I am in a new place. It is the summer of 2006. We still live in the condo. Aalia and Adam still go to their Christian school. We still attend our home church. I still work for the church and Mr. Richard. Things are changing at my home church. The enemy has been allowed to cause a wedge. Whispers of a division.

The Lord said to Cain, "Why are you angry? And why has your countenance fallen? If you do well, will not your countenance be lifted up? And if you do not do well, sin is crouching at the door; and its desire is for you, but you must master it."

Genesis 4:6-7 (NASB)

"Sin is crouching at the door." Countenance is a person's face or facial expression. "Lift our eyes up to the Lord," is a phrase meaning to pray and communicate with God. We have taken our eyes off of Him, and we have started looking at our circumstances.

Things are also changing in me. I am no longer content with listening to bullet point sermons and foo-foo phrases starting with the same letter of the alphabet. I like my Sunday school class, but I want more. I am hungry. What two trips to Israel taught me (besides a whole lot about pretty much everything) is that the Bible is an incredible source of inspiration and illumination. I am studying the Bible in a whole new way.

Let me explain it like this. I now pick up my Bible and take one book at a time. I start with the smallest book, and I pick apart the whole book. I look up the Greek and the Hebrew. If there is a word I don't understand, I pray for help to understand. I study the history and who wrote it. I answer the where and the why the who and the what and the when. I seek and find, and I grow. I slowly move up from the smallest books, which have trained me for the larger books. I write a lot in my Bible. When I returned to work for Mr. Richard, he gave me a new blue study Bible with lots of room in the margins for my notes.

One of the books that changed me was the Book of Ruth. This book encouraged me and gave me hope in my journey to follow God. I know what you are thinking, the "M" word. Well, trust me, that is so NOT what I was thinking! Marriage is never on my mind. I guess because I daily live with the consequences of disobedience and my first marriage. I really should have listened when God said, "Don't do it!" And then again, when He would later say, "I told you, don't do it." Now the idea of marriage does not enter into my world of thought. I joke that it won't be until the day I hear Him quote Michael Jordan and say, "Just do it." I think that I am pretty safe because the God of the Universe does not need to quote Michael Jordan.

But back to the Book of Ruth. It is a story of love and dedication, obedience and integrity, but also a story of the future. It is a blessing. The Book of Ruth is an illustration of how the body of Christ is called to respond to the unconditional covenant and its unchangeable truth of being a blessing to Israel and being blessed by Israel. This is good stuff, people!

Now it came about in the days when the judges governed, that there was a famine in the land. And a certain man of Bethlehem in Judah went to sojourn in the land of Moab with his wife and his two sons.

Ruth 1:1 (NASB)

Bethlehem means "House of Bread." Bethlehem is known for its large fields that are divided into sections where crops of barley grow in the spring and wheat grows in the summer. Bethlehem represents a place of God's provision. Bread is life. In the desert during the time in the wilderness, they ate only the Manna from Heaven. If they obeyed God and ate it, then they lived. The place of provision for life is the same place where Jesus is born, Bethlehem. If you are a believer, then He is your provision for eternal life as it says in John 14:6. In John 6:35, Jesus says that He is the Bread of Life. Bread also represents God's Word. In Deuteronomy 8:3, it says, "Man does not live by bread alone, but man lives by everything that proceeds out of the mouth of the LORD." In Matthew 6:11, we say, "Give us this day our daily bread," meaning that we need to eat both physically and spiritually to have a life.

There is a famine in the land. A famine can happen because of drought and the lack of rain, but it can also happen for many other reasons. Famine can also represent the spiritual condition of the people. The Word of God is not a part of the life of the Jewish people at this time. This spiritual condition leaves a person both physically and spiritually hungry. I can relate. I am right there. I am very hungry!

So famine has caused a certain man of Bethlehem to leave Bethlehem and go to Moab. He chose to dwell as a sojourner, live as a foreigner, rather than live in Israel. I looked up the word "Moab" and found the definition included "the original meaning of Moab is unknown and the word Moab is foreign to Hebrew." Should one go to a place that is foreign if God Himself has not sent them? This is a dangerous place. Moab is a real place where bad things can happen to good people. When people leave a place where God has placed them (like Bethlehem) and provided for them and go to a new place because they give in to their "lusts,"* then that is a dangerous place to be. It is a place outside of the will of God. When people are hungry, both physically and spiritually, they will look for bread in strange places. Be careful. You should expect trouble when you leave a place of "inheritance" for a place with no "inheritance." Inheritance means a future, people!

The name of the man was Elimelech, and the name of his wife, Naomi; and the names of his two sons were Mahlon and Chilion, Ephrathites of Bethlehem in Judah. Now they entered the land of Moab and remained there.

Ruth 1:2 (NASB)

The man's name, Elimelech, means "My God is King." His wife's name, Naomi, means "Pleasant." His two son's names, Mahlon and Chilion, mean "Sickly" and "Wasting Away." Names are very important! Did you even read my second book?

Now the family is in Moab. Moab was the incestuous son of Lot and his elder daughter. Moab was the father of the

Moabites. The Moabites live in Moab and now so does this Hebrew family.

Then Elimelech, Naomi's husband, died; and she was left with her two sons. They took for themselves Moabite women as wives; the name of one was Orpah and the name of the other Ruth. And they lived there about ten years. Then both Mahlon and Chilion also died, and the woman was bereft of her two children and her husband.

Ruth 1:3-5 (NASB)

Elimelech is disobedient and leaves his inherited, God-given land, Bethlehem, and takes his family to Moab. Disobedience has consequences, people! He dies there leaving his wife and two sons. They both take wives that are not Jewish. They are both Moabites. That means they are NOT Hebrews. That means that the sons are disobedient like their father. With names like "sickly" and "wasting away," you would think they would be a bit more careful! Names are also important in that Orpah means "back of neck" or "stiff-necked" and Ruth means "clinging one" or "friend." The two sons live "ten" years in Moab and die. Ten in Hebrew is the number of "completion." The time of disobedience is ending, and it's time to return to Bethlehem.

Then she (Naomi) arose with her daughters-in-law that she might return from the land of Moab, for she had heard in the land of Moab that the LORD had visited His people in giving them food. So she departed from the place where she was, and her two daughters –in-law with her; and they went on the way to return to the land of Judah.

Ruth 1:6-7 (NASB)

At this point, Naomi is not thinking or acting like a person of faith. She is making her decision on returning to the land of Judah based on what she has "heard." Never assume that the obvious is the right thing to do. Always seek to know God's will in any situation. Naomi has heard that God cares for and is paying attention to the needs of His people. Both of her two daughters-in-law start out to leave with her.

And Naomi said to her two daughters-in-law, "Go, return each of you to her mother's house. May the LORD deal kindly with you as you have dealt with the dead and with me. May the LORD grant that you may find rest, each in the house of her husband." Then she kissed them, and they lifted up their voices and wept. And they said to her, "No, but we will surely return with you to your people." But Naomi said, "Return, my daughters. Why should you go with me? Have I yet sons in my womb, that they may be your husbands? Return, my daughters! Go, for I am too old to have a husband. If I said I have hope, if I should even have a husband tonight and also bear sons, would you, therefore, wait until they were grown? Would you, therefore, refrain from marrying? No, my daughters; for it is harder for me than for you, for the hand of the LORD has gone forth against me."

Ruth 1:8-13 (NASB)

Three times Naomi says to her daughters-in-law, "return," meaning to turn back. Three in Hebrew is the number of verification and unity. Three times Naomi discourages her daughters-in-law. Depressed people give poor advice. Naomi says that she has no hope of a future marriage or children. Naomi has no hope for her future because she cannot see past her current situation of having no husband and no sons. Her thinking is blurred from crying, and her faith is weak because she cannot see a future beyond the death of her sons. Naomi trusts too much in what she "hears" and what she "sees." She does not see the Lord in her circumstances and tells her daughters that "the hand of the LORD has gone forth against me." In Hebrew, the phrase "hand of the Lord" means the power of the Lord.

And they lifted up their voices and wept again, and Orpah kissed her mother-in-law, but Ruth clung to her.

Ruth 1:14 (NASB)

Orpah's reaction is to serve herself. She reacts with great words, gestures, and a "kiss." Then she departs. She returns to her old ways and her people.

Then she (Naomi) said, "Behold, your sister-in-law has gone back to her people and her gods; return after your sister-in-law." But Ruth said, "Do not urge me to leave you or turn back from following you; for where you go, I will go, and where you lodge, I will lodge. Your people shall be my people, and your God, my God. Where you die, I will die, and there I will be buried. Thus may the LORD do to me, and worse if anything but death parts you and me." When she (Naomi) saw that she (Ruth) was determined to go with her, she said no more to her.

Ruth 1:15-18 (NASB)

Ruth's reaction is to serve others. She reacts with great works, gestures, and a kiss then clings to Naomi. She stays and goes with Naomi. She turns from her old ways and her people. It also says "behold." It did not say that when referring to Orpah. It only says that to Ruth. "Behold" means "to see or to perceive." To behold is to fix one's eyes upon, to see with attention, or to observe with care. To behold is to see or to observe someone or something, especially of remarkable or impressive nature. Behold means to pay attention because God is up to something good! Are you sure you read the other two books, people?

So they both went until they came to Bethlehem. And when they had come to Bethlehem, all the city was stirred because of them, and the women said, "Is this Naomi?" She said to them, "Do not call me Naomi; call me Mara, for the Almighty has dealt very bitterly with me. I went out full, but the LORD has brought me back empty. Why do you call me Naomi, since the LORD has witnessed against me and the Almighty has afflicted me?" So Naomi returned, and with her Ruth the Moabitess, her daughter-in-law, who returned from the land of Moab. And they came to Bethlehem at the beginning of the barley harvest.

Ruth 1:19-22 (NASB)

Ruth says a most beautiful phrase in verse sixteen. "Your people shall be my people, and your God, my God." The love relationship between the Jewish people (Naomi), and the non-Jewish (Ruth, the Gentiles, who represents everyone else,

15

including the Moabites) is an important idea. The Gentile who believes in the God of Israel will not let go of the Jewish people, no matter how embittered they seem. Ruth enters Bethlehem changed by the God of Naomi. Naomi, however, enters bitter, broken, and bankrupt. Oops. I used all words that begin with the letter "b." Ugh!

Naomi tells those who greet her, those who know her from ten years ago, those who have not forgotten her, those who know her as a wealthy woman with a full home that she has changed from "pleasant" to "bitter." Mara means "bitter." Naomi is not the same woman. Bitterness and sorrow can blur the perception of what God is doing, has done, and will do. Instead, her bitterness does not allow her to see her disobedience in following circumstances that her flesh ears "hear" and her flesh eyes "see." It is far easier to point the blame toward the Almighty than to acknowledge your fleshiness in your circumstances. Sin equals death.

One more note. Naomi and Ruth left Moab. When you leave Moab, it becomes your "past." Leave your past, your disobedience, and your flesh behind, and cross the Jordan River to the place where God is leading you. If you do this, then you will discover the key to your future and your purpose. To do this, you must be at the right place at the right time and be sensitive to the leading of the Holy Spirit. Return to God's provision, and you will be blessed. Can I get an Amen! Ruth understood that. That is why she was willing to leave Moab in her past and turn from her old ways and her old gods. Repentance is powerful! She desires to live in the Bread of Life!

Now Naomi had a kinsman of her husband, a man of great wealth, of the family of Elimelech, whose name was Boaz. And Ruth the Moabitess said to Naomi, "Please let me go to the field and glean among the ears of grain after one in whose sight I may find favor." And she said to her, "Go, my daughter." So she departed and went and gleaned in the field after the reapers; and she happened to come to the portion of the field belonging to Boaz, who was of the family of Elimelech.

Ruth 2:1-3 (NASB)

Naomi is now once again living in the land of Israel. She is now back in the place of her inheritance. A place where her husband had inherited land, a place of a family member of the family of Elimelech who is wealthy and named Boaz. In Hebrew, Boaz means "in him is strength." Her past is still defining Ruth by being called a "Moabitess." To those around her, she seems to be a foreigner in her new land. The world will do that to you. So will the church. You may be a new member of the family of God and, while you recognize the change and begin to change, others choose not to. They choose to define you by your past, by your relationship to Moab. I read this and decided to no longer refer to myself as a former Muslim but as a believer in Christ Jesus. It takes a while and a lot of growth, but you will get bold for Jesus, and you will no longer need that old Moabitess definition!

Ruth, respecting Naomi's positioning, asks permission to go and gather grain among those that will show her favor, meaning grace and acceptance. Naomi recognizes the change in Ruth because she no longer defines her as "daughter-in-law" but as "daughter." She is family! It's good to be a part of God's family!

Now behold, Boaz came from Bethlehem and said to the reapers, "May the LORD be with you." And they said to him, "May the LORD bless you." Then Boaz said to his servant who was in charge of the reapers "Whose young woman is this?" The servant in charge of the reapers replied, "She is the young Moabite woman who returned with Naomi from the land of Moab. And she said, 'Please let me glean and gather after the reapers among the sheaves.' Thus she came and has remained from the morning until now; she has been sitting in the house for a little while." Then Boaz said to Ruth, "Listen carefully, my daughter. Do not go to glean in another field; furthermore, do not go on from this one, but stay here with my maids. Let your eyes be on the field which they reap, and go after them. Indeed, I have commanded the servants not to touch you. When you are thirsty, go to the water jars and drink from what the servants draw." Then she fell on her face, bowing to the ground and said to him, "Why have I found favor in your sight that you should take notice of me, since I am a foreigner?"

Ruth 2:4-10 (NASB)

First, "behold" starts out this section. This is good stuff, people! Behold means that God is up to something good! Boaz starts by coming to the field. God positions him to bless those who are in his field and those in his field return the blessing. The word "bless" in Hebrew is "barak," which means "to kneel, to bless, to enrich another" and "bending at the knee." His positioning allows him to see Ruth, who has also been positioned by God to be in his field. He takes note of her and notes the integrity in which she goes about her work.

Boaz says, "Listen." This word in Hebrew is "shema," which means, "to hear and obey." It means more than just listen or hear, but act and obey. He calls her close to tell her that he wants her to work protected in his fields, gives good advice to her, and tells her that she should drink from the water jars when she is thirsty. It is good to be in the position that God places you because you will be safe, secure, and provided for!

Ruth is amazed that Boaz recognizes and takes notice of her. Ruth forgets to whom she belongs and labels herself a foreigner, and acts like one, by bowing her face to the ground. Pagans bow their faces to the ground. I know; I used to be one! In the Bible, the Hebrews respectfully "take to their knees," except when the Lord stood before them. That is when they went prostrate to the ground because of the glory of God.

Bunny trail time – I get a kick out of those who say that "the glory of God came down in the church today." To which I ask, "Were you still standing?" "Yes," they reply, "We sang and sang, and the preaching went on and on," etc. I always argue that one. "It's just an emotion," I say, "a feeling you were experiencing," because I double-dog-dare anyone to remain standing when the glory of the Lord comes down on you! I know because I have had that glory melt me on a balcony in the courtroom back when the Lord told me, "I told you, don't do it." It was as if I had bones made of Jell-O, and I just melted like snow in the desert! I plan to bow down only and ever to my Kinsman Redeemer, Jesus Christ! But, off this bunny trail and back to Ruth! Ruth is positioned in humility. She doesn't know it yet, but she has just bowed down to her kinsman redeemer. Boaz is a kinsman redeemer. Boaz is a picture of Christ to the Bride of Christ, His church!

Boaz replied to her, "All you have done for your mother-in-law after the death of your husband has been fully reported to me, and how you left your father and your mother and the land of your birth, and came to a people that you did not previously know. May the LORD reward your work, and your wages be full from the LORD, the God of Israel, under whose wings you have come to seek refuge." Then she said, "I have found favor in your sight, my lord, for you have comforted me and indeed have spoken kindly to your maidservant, though I am not like one of your maidservants."

Ruth 2:11-13 (NASB)

Boaz recognizes her as family and not as a stranger. Boaz also recognizes her deeds, even if Ruth does not realize that he knows. We often think that no one sees what good we have done; but trust me, dear ones, our Kinsman Redeemer, Jesus Christ, does. He is always watching, and if we are willing to be positioned to receive His blessings, He will open the storehouses! He says, "a people you did not previously know." That word "know" is the Hebrew word "yada" which means to intimately know and understand. He recognizes that she is positioned in the protective refuge of being under the wings (covering) of the Lord God of Israel. She is positioned in hope! She, in turn, recognizes that he has spoken from the heart and in peace.

At mealtime, Boaz said to her, "Come here, that you may eat of the bread and dip your piece of bread in the vinegar." So she sat beside the reapers; and he served her roasted grain, and she ate and was satisfied and had some left. When she rose to glean, Boaz commanded his servants, saying, "Let her glean even among the sheaves, and do not insult her. Also, you shall purposely pull out for her some grain from the bundles and leave it that she may glean, and do not rebuke her." So she gleaned in the field until evening. Then she beat out what she had gleaned, and it was about an ephah of barley. She took it up and went into the city, and her mother-in-law saw what she

had gleaned. She also took it out and gave Naomi what she had left after she was satisfied. Her mother-in-law then said to her, "Where did you glean today and where did you work? May he who took notice of you be blessed." So she told her mother-in-law with whom she had worked and said, "The name of the man with whom I worked today is Boaz."

Ruth 2:14-19 (NASB)

During the meal, Boaz blesses her in a 30-fold manner. He blesses her with "just enough." When your Kinsman Redeemer chooses to bless you, He will position you to be filled up to satisfaction and overflowing. You will always have enough if you are filled up and are satisfied with Him. Boaz then goes on to command with authority and appoint his workers to bless her by purposely leaving behind grain. She is hard-working, and Boaz helps her by commanding that portions be left behind. It allows her to be blessed with more than she would normally be able to pick up. At the command to leave purposeful handfuls behind, she is being blessed in a 60-fold manner. Her needs are met and the blessings are on purpose. She has enough and some to share.

She bends down to pick up the grain and as she does, she, in turn, can bless Naomi by returning home with a large portion of the grain. Her willingness to kneel, to bend, and to enrich another is a blessing. Remember what "barak" means? Naomi recognized that Ruth had more than a normal work day's worth of grain. She "saw" with her own eyes the blessing of the larger portion of the grain. This Gentile woman named Ruth kneels down to bless the Jewish woman named Naomi. God has a plan, and it is a good one! Full of plenty and blessings!

If God positions you and you are obedient in that positioning, you will be blessed. But also note that Ruth didn't just sit around and let the purposeful handouts fall in her lap nor did she ask others to get them for her. Ruth worked hard. She dedicated her work for Naomi's benefit and concentrated on the "task" and not the "task master." Love the work God gives you while you wait on the Lord. Enjoy this time of purposeful handfuls!

Naomi said to her daughter-in-law, "May he be blessed of the LORD who has not withdrawn his kindness to the living and to the dead." Again Naomi said to her, "The man is our relative, he is one of our closest relatives." Then Ruth the Moabitess said, "Furthermore, he said to me, 'You should stay close to my servants until they have finished all my harvest.'" Naomi said to Ruth her daughter-in-law, "It is good, my daughter, that you go out with his maids, so that others do not fall upon you in another field." So she (Ruth) stayed close by the maids of Boaz in order to glean until the end of the barley harvest and the wheat harvest. And she lived with her mother-in-law.

Ruth 2:20-23 (NASB)

Naomi sees that Boaz has shown grace to Ruth. Grace is unmerited. It is a divine blessing that comes from God to you. Sometimes in the form of grain and sometimes in the form of the Son of Man who died on the cross for all. Naomi sees that Boaz has shown favor to Ruth. Favor is unearned. It is blessings given to you by men. This blessing source is from God, but the flow comes through a man. Ruth is truthful to Naomi and repeats the authoritative instructions she received from Boaz and Naomi confirms that Ruth should obey. Ruth enters a "season," more specifically, the seasons of the barley and the wheat harvests, working hard and being submissive to the authority of both Naomi and Boaz. Stay in your position until that season is "kawlal" which in Hebrew means ends, completes, or is accomplished.

Then Naomi her mother-in-law said to her, "My daughter, shall I not seek security for you, that it may be well with you? Now is not Boaz our kinsman, with whose maids you were? Behold, he winnows barley at the threshing floor tonight. Wash yourself, therefore, and anoint yourself and put on your best clothes, and go down to the threshing floor; but do not make yourself known to the man until he has finished eating and drinking. It shall be when he lies down, that you shall notice the place where he lies, and you shall go and uncover his feet and lie down; then he will tell you what you should do." She (Ruth) said to her, "All that you say I will do." So she went

down to the threshing floor and did according to all that her mother-in-law had commanded her.

Ruth 3:1-6 (NASB)

Naomi is now the one that sits positioned. She knows the rules and the traditions of the Jewish people, her people. She shares them with her family and passes down the rules and traditions to her daughter Ruth. She sits in a position to be a blessing. If Ruth obeys her mother-in-law, then she will be blessed. The Book of Ephesians has a wonderful promise for those who obey their parents in the Lord, for this is right, and it may be well with you, and you may live long on the earth. This is the first commandment with a promise! So Naomi tells Ruth to get "prepared" by cleansing, anointing, and changing clothes. She commands her to "get thee to the floor." Ruth obeys.

This is not just any floor but a threshing floor. This is the floor where the chaff is separated from the fruit of the grain. This is the floor that exposes the chaff which represents pride, rebellion, and stubbornness. This is the floor that exposes the fruit, which represents a future both because it will feed in the present and feed with the seeds for the future. This is the floor that can be a floor of a major breakthrough.

Just remember that, before a major breakthrough, there will be a breakdown. The chaff is deceptive. Chaff looks good, and it is harvested along with the grain. Only on the threshing floor, through the winnowing or sifting by the wind will the chaff or deception be revealed. The chaff will blow away in the wind while the fruit is heavy and falls back to the threshing floor to be gathered up.

The word wind in Hebrew is "ruach" which means wind, breath, spirit. When you add "HaKodesh" meaning "the holy" to "ruach." You get "Ruach HaKodesh" which is the Holy Spirit. Winnowing is like being spiritually tested. Your faith will be sifted. You will be sifted by the Holy Spirit. This process will increase your faith and increase your character because you will look more like Christ.

But Satan sends tests too. Be careful that the enemy of your soul is not sending you something that "looks good." Take care not to be deceived by the evil one because he would love for you to make the mistake of choosing the chaff over the grain. The chaff has no future. It will be gathered up and burned. This process will decrease your faith and decrease your character, and you will look more like the enemy of your soul than Christ.

A threshing floor is a place of battle. This character-building process of winnowing directly affects your future. In John's Gospel, Jesus states that the enemy of your soul "comes only to steal, kill and destroy!" The reason you sleep on the threshing floor is that your "future" is at risk. You do not want to leave your threshing floor unguarded because the enemy will come to steal your grain, kill your current crops, and destroy your future crops by not leaving you seed for your future planting and harvest. But in the same passage, Jesus says, "I came that they may have life, and have it abundantly!" So the fruit will be gathered up and put into His barn where He has a hope and a plan. An eternal plan!

Notice also that Naomi warns her to not "make herself known" to him until the right time. The Hebrew word is "yada" which means to intimately know and understand; it is also how Adam "knew" Eve. Don't rush God's timing and plans. Do things in His order. Ruth needs to do things in the order that Naomi tells her, including being obedient to wait until he is finished eating and drinking, meaning that he will then be full and satisfied. She needs to obey and watch where he lies down. And then obey by doing just what Naomi says by uncovering his feet and lying down and waiting for Boaz to give her instructions. Ruth has to wait for Boaz to give her the next step. Ruth is in an intimate position. She is in a humble position. She is in a waiting position. Her actions require a response from Boaz. Waiting is a hard position to be in. Do you have the fortitude to wait on the Lord for a response?

When Boaz had eaten and drunk and his heart was merry, he went to lie down at the end of the heap of grain; and she came secretly, and uncovered his feet and lay down. It happened in the middle of the night that the man was startled and bent forward; and behold, a woman was lying at his feet. He said,

"Who are you?" And she answered, "I am Ruth your maid. So spread your covering over your maid, for you are a close relative." Then he said, "May you be blessed of the LORD, my daughter. You have shown your last kindness to be better than the first by not going after young men, whether poor or rich. Now, my daughter, do not fear. I will do for you whatever you ask, for all my people in the city know that you are a woman of excellence. Now it is true that I am a close relative; however, there is a relative closer than I. Remain this night, and when morning comes, if he will redeem you, good; let him redeem you. But if he does not wish to redeem you, then I will redeem you, as the LORD lives. Lie down until morning."

So she lay at his feet until morning and rose before one could recognize another; and he said, "Let it not be known that the woman came to the threshing floor." And again he said, "Give me the cloak that is on you and hold it." So she held it, and he measured six measures of barley and laid it on her. Then she went into the city. When she came to her mother-in-law, she said, "How did it go, my daughter?" And she told her all that the man (Boaz) had done for her. She said, "These six measures of barley he gave to me, for he said 'Do not go to your mother-in-law empty-handed.'" Then she (Naomi) said, "Wait, my daughter, until you know how the matter turns out; for the man will not rest until he has settled it today."

Ruth 3:7-18 (NASB)

Ruth obeyed and waited. Did you see the "behold" when Boaz found her at his feet? It doesn't get any better than this, people! This is good stuff! Boaz also knows the customs and rules of his people. The Jewish people have a plan for how one marries to keep the family line intact. Boaz knows this plan, is honest with Ruth and tells her that there is one person closer than he is. To protect her honor, he wants her to leave the threshing floor before she can be recognized. He sends her away with six measures of barley. The number six in Hebrew means man and is one number off of perfection, which is the number seven.

Then comes my second favorite phrase in the Book of Ruth. Naomi tells Ruth to wait. I love how Sylvia Gunter writes in her daily devotional, "Be Still, My Daughter." Her paraphrase of Ruth 3:18 says, "Sit still, My daughter, the apple of My eye, waiting as long as it takes, until you learn (know, perceive, understand, discern, and distinguish as truth) how the matter, thing, question, or cause will turn out, because surely the Man Christ Jesus, your Kinsman-Redeemer, will not by any means be idle, or silent, or have any peace until He finishes His purposes, working until the job is done, in His eternal now."**

Chapter four has Boaz going to the gate of the city to speak with the close relative who is the one to have the first opportunity to redeem Ruth. This man is unnamed because of his lack of faith. This man chooses not to redeem Ruth, going against the commandments of the Lord. He chooses the world's ways and not God's way. He worries that he will jeopardize his inheritance. This man thinks that it will cost too much because he will have to pay top dollar for the land. He will have to produce an heir that will not have his name. This heir will redeem the family line of Elimelech and not his own. This heir will one day own the land, and this unnamed man will be out his investment. In other words, "What's in it for me?" The unnamed man of little faith missed the opportunity for God to bless his future.

Boaz being the very picture of an honorable kinsman redeemer announces to the elders and all the people that he plans to redeem Ruth as his wife.

So Boaz took Ruth, and she became his wife, and he went in to her. And the LORD enabled her to conceive, and she gave birth to a son. Then the women said to Naomi, "Blessed is the LORD who has not left you without a redeemer today, and may his name become famous in Israel. May he also be to you a restorer of life and a sustainer of your old age; for your daughter-in-law, who loves you and is better to you than seven sons, has given birth to him." Then Naomi took the child and laid him in her lap, and became his nurse. The neighbor women gave him a name, saying, "A son has been born to Naomi!" So they named him Obed. He is the father of Jesse, the father of David.

Ruth 4:13-17 (NASB)

Boaz redeems both Ruth and Naomi, and Obed is born. Obed's name means "servant" in Hebrew. And by the way, if you have not figured it out, Boaz and then Obed are the 100-fold blessings for Ruth. Her marriage to Boaz followed by the birth of her son are total provision and blessing, and she can be a blessing to many others. In fact, generations and generations of others because of Jesus!

And Naomi, remember how she wanted to be called bitter? Mara, in the form of "Marah," was introduced in the wilderness. Israel came to the bitter waters of Marah. You cannot drink the bitter water. Moses then throws a piece of wood into the water to heal it and change it from bitter to sweet and drinkable. The cross of Christ is that piece of wood that changes our bitter to sweet. And as far as Naomi goes, I don't think anyone can remain bitter with a sweet baby on their lap. What the women of Bethlehem tell her is a prophetic word. This one will become famous in all of Israel!

Naomi is a picture of the Jewish people married to God. Her sons, Mahlon "sickly" and Chilion "wasting away," reflect the spiritual condition of the Jewish people at that time. Ruth is the picture of the church, who is adopted into the family of God through repentance and by the Kinsman Redeemer. Boaz is a prophetic depiction of the Messiah. Through the mutual relationship and mutual blessings of Naomi the Jew and Ruth the Gentile, the ultimate Kinsman Redeemer will be born into this world. Jesus is our Kinsman Redeemer. He comes from the genealogy listed in the Book of Matthew which names Boaz and Ruth. Only five women are mentioned in this genealogy. Just five. What an honor! What faith! What a wonderful God!

Looking back, this relationship brings about the first coming of Jesus, and it will bring about the second coming of Jesus. We just need to get on board with God's plan and God's way. We need to be a blessing to the Jewish people and in turn, the Jewish people will be a blessing to us. Why do you think anti-Semitism flows in our world of flesh? Did you not learn anything, people? Because of the enemy of your soul, Satan, and borrowing from Maggie Smith's line in Harry Potter; "You might as well use his name, he is going to try and kill you." Satan wants to delay the return of Jesus. He wants to steal, kill, and destroy.

Our inheritance is our future which is the Kingdom of God!

Then the LORD said to Moses, "Behold, I will rain bread from heaven for you; and the people shall go out and gather a day's portion every day, that I may test them, whether or not they will walk in My instruction."

Exodus 16:4 (NASB)

Now after Jesus was born in Bethlehem of Judea in the days of Herod the king, magi from the east arrived in Jerusalem, saying, "Where is He who has been born King of the Jews? For we saw His star in the east and have come to worship Him."

Matthew 2:1-2 (NASB)

Jesus said to him, "I am the way, and the truth, and the life; no one comes to the Father but through Me."

John 14:6 (NASB)

Jesus said to them, "I am the bread of life; he who comes to Me will not hunger, and he who believes in Me will never thirst."

John 6:35 (NASB)

You shall remember all the way which the LORD your God has led you in the wilderness these forty years, that He might humble you, testing you, to know what was in your heart, whether you would keep His commandments or not. He humbled you and let you be hungry, and fed you with manna which you did not know, nor did your fathers know, that He might make you understand that man does not live by bread alone, but man lives by everything that proceeds out of the mouth of the LORD. Your clothing did not wear out on you, nor did your foot swell these forty years. Thus you are to know in your heart that the LORD your God was disciplining you just as a man disciplines his son. Therefore, you shall keep the

commandments of the LORD your God, to walk in His ways and to fear Him.

Deuteronomy 8:2-6 (NASB)

Pray, then, in this way: 'Our Father who is in heaven, Hallowed be Your name. Your kingdom come. Your will be done, on earth as it is in heaven. Give us this day our daily bread. And forgive us our debts, as we also have forgiven our debtors. And do not lead us into temptation, but deliver us from evil. For Yours is the kingdom and the power and the glory forever. Amen.'

Matthew 6:9-13 (NASB)

Thus both the daughters of Lot were with child by their father. The firstborn bore a son, and called his name Moab; he is the father of the Moabites to this day.

Genesis 19:36-37 (NASB)

Children, obey your parents in the Lord, for this is right. Honor your father and mother (which is the first commandment with a promise), so that it may be well with you, and that you may live long on the earth.

Ephesians 6:1-2 (NSAB)

The thief comes only to steal and kill and destroy; I came that they may have life, and have it abundantly.

John 10:10

*I will explain lust later in the book.

**This is taken from *Prayer Essentials For Living In His Presence,* Vol. 2, p. 81-82, © 2000 by Sylvia Gunter.

Purposeful Handfuls

After I got saved in 1995, I was still a single mother. But I was a saved single mother! Somehow by the grace of God and through the favor of man, the children and I were always provided for. We always had "just enough." Now that did not mean fancy anything. No coffee runs or eating out, no entertainment budget or brand named clothes. We were well taken care of. We had a home. We had food. We had a vehicle. We had health insurance. We had what we needed.

Things changed when I returned "home" in 2002 to work at the church in which I was saved. I believe that the children and I were in a season of "purposeful handfuls." The fourth chapter of the Book of Mark talks about the thirty, sixty, and hundredfold.

And those are the ones on whom seed was sown on the good soil; and they hear the word and accept it and bear fruit, thirty, sixty, and a hundredfold.

Mark 4:20 (NASB)

Looking back, I am amazed at how God provided for us when I technically did not make much money. Somehow, by the grace of God and through the favor of man, the children and I were always provided for. That did not mean that I sat back and ate chocolates on my couch. I worked. I worked a lot. I worked at the church, and I worked several small part-time jobs such as wedding coordinating and childcare. The Bible says, "If you want to eat, you need to work!" I read an article on the amount of money you make in a year and what that number meant as far as being classified as "low income." I asked my son if it bothered him to be low income. He replied, "We are poor?" How great is our God that my children did not realize that we were "low income!"

Now I am going to bold this part. Usually I only "bold" the Word of God but I feel very strongly that you, the reader, do not miss this next part!

Please don't read thirty fold, sixty fold, or hundredfold and think it to be "financial blessings." This is not prosperity gospel, people! Read Mark 4:20 again.

And those are the ones (the people) **on whom seed** (the Word of God) **was sown on the good soil** (the Word of God gets into people)**; and they hear** (listen) **the word** (Word of God) **and accept** (respond and be in one accord with God's will) **it** (the seed, God's Word) **and bear** (produce) **fruit** (more seeds, good works, blessing others, putting God's Word in action, magnifying and manifesting the Word of God)**, thirty** (measure of producing fruit)**, sixty** (measure of producing fruit that is more than 30)**, and a hundredfold** (measure of producing fruit that is more than thirty, sixty, but is complete meaning instead of the expected 90 as the next mathematical step but with even more).

Mark 4:20 (SNV) (Shahe Nahler's Version)

Why do you think that I was financially taken care of? It's not because I learned to tithe or gave a ministry a donation. It's not because I did some good deed and it multiplied. It is not because of random acts of kindness (there is nothing "random" about God). It has nothing to do with paying it forward! It's not because I figured out the magic door to step into or that I have the secret key to attaining the secret to get "more." It's not because of anything I did…except…wait for it…I responded to the Word of God. Wait, what?

Response.

I know what you are thinking, "That's it? You responded to the Word of God?"

Yes, and it didn't involve my checkbook, a credit card, or the sweaty, yelling, begging for your money preacher on TV. Don't be fooled by those that teach part of the Word of God. You can't skip around and expect to get the whole picture. Don't just listen to God's Word. Listen to it and read it! Don't just read a Bible verse. Read a Bible verse and read some more. Read chapters, Read entire books. Study all of the books of the Bible.

Study the Word of God! Meditate on the Word of God! Memorize the Word of God!

Now go a step further and put God's Word into action. Eat every last piece of the Bread of Life. Let it nourish you. Let it strengthen you. Let it grow you from the inside out. The Word of God can heal you from the inside out. Now take the Bread of Life and use your new muscles and put His Word into actions. Walk and pray in a neighborhood or in a nation that does not know Jesus! Lift your arms and fill up a food box for someone and then feed them both physically and spiritually. Curb your tongue and make it less about your opinion and more about what God's Word says. I can go on and on, but these are just a few examples.

How do I know that response is the key? Backup in Mark chapter 4. Jesus is teaching on the Sea of Galilee. A large crowd has gathered, and they are listening. Jesus has positioned Himself on a boat in the water. Why? Because He has positioned Himself so that more people can "hear" Him. But this does not mean just "listen" to Him. It means that they can "hear" Him and "respond" to Him. They can respond to His teachings by applying His teachings to their lives. They can experience what He is teaching about when they apply God's Word to their lives.

It next mentions that the sower went out to sow. What did the sower sow? Seed. What is the seed? Down in Mark 4:14, it says, "The sower sows the word." The seed is the Word of God.

The sower will sow seed on four different types of ground. These four types of "ground" represent four different types of people and their **response** to the seed (the Word of God). Why four? Well, four in Hebrew represents things of the earth, like the four corners of the earth, four directions of the wind, or four seasons of growth. But the number four can also refer to a global nature. In other words, globally, every person will fall into one of these four types of ground or responses to God's Word in their life when the seed (Word of God) is sown.

The first ground (person), the seed is sown, and it falls beside the road. The seed (Word of God) sits on top of the ground and is not a part of the ground. It never goes into the ground (people). When the seed lands on the surface of the ground (people), it is easy for the birds to come and eat it up. No fruit is produced.

The second ground (person), the seed is sown, and it falls on rocky ground where it does not have much soil. The seed immediately springs up, but it has no roots to maintain and grow. The sun comes up and scorches the seed (the seed is dry and not watered). Because there are no roots, the newly planted seed dies. No fruit is produced.

The third ground (person), the seed is sown, and it falls among the thorns, and the thorns come up and choke it. The newly planted seed dies. No fruit is produced.

The fourth ground (person), the seed is sown, and it falls on good ground. The newly planted seed makes roots and grows. The plant continues to grow, first in a blade, then the head, and then mature grain in the head (Mark 4:28). The seed becomes a mature plant that produces fruit (more seeds). The seed yields (gives up) and produces a crop, and that crop can be harvested in thirty, sixty, or a hundredfold.

Jesus goes on to explain the parable, not to the whole crowd by the Sea of Galilee, but to a few others and His disciples. The ones that pushed forward and responded to His teachings.

These four types of grounds are the people and how they handle and respond to the Word of God, which is the seed that is sown.

The first ground is not able to receive the seed (Word of God); therefore, no response happens. No fruit is produced. Mark 4:15 says, that Satan steals the seed (Word of God) from this ground (person). Don't forget, Satan comes to steal, kill, and destroy, people! Don't go about your days doing what you think is best because you may think that you are in control of your life. Instead, you have allowed Satan himself to be present in your circumstances.

The second ground receives the seed (Word of God). They hear the Word of God and respond immediately with joy (Mark 4:16). But because there is no firm root (foundation in the Word of God), the response to the seed is temporary. "When affliction and persecution arise *because of the word,* immediately they fall away." Did you notice the important part? The seed is the Word of God. When the seed is sown in a person (ground), and a person responds like the "rocky ground" in that their response is temporary. That person falls away because of the *affliction and persecution that arise because of God's Word.* It is all about God's Word! This person's response can be measured by the evidence it produces. No crop is formed and no fruit is produced. The seed dies before it can ever grow and produce fruit. Don't go about your days doing what you think is your best for God only to immediately leave His ways when His ways do not agree with your ways. Instead, let go of your old ways and let God's way take hold.

The third ground receives the seed (Word of God). They hear the Word of God and respond, but the external worries of the world and the external deceitfulness of riches and the internal desires for other things get in the way of their response to the Word of God. The seed's growth is choked. It becomes unfruitful. Don't go about your days focusing on the things of this world. Instead, be focused on the Kingdom of God.

The fourth ground receives the seed (Word of God). They hear the Word of God and accept it and bear fruit! Praise the Lord! Sometimes I wonder if we frustrate God. It's a good thing I am not God because, if I were to sow seed, and three out of four types of ground did not produce fruit, I would give up before I got to the fourth. Flood the place! Wipe them out! Maybe that's why I wrote, "Praise the Lord!" Because by the time you read about the fourth ground, it seems about time that someone (some ground) accepted and responded to that seed! That precious seed that is the Word of God!

This fourth ground is the person that hears God's Word and applies it to and in their lives. This person has the Word of God in them so that they can be positioned to be in accord with the Will of

God. I can't emphasize this enough. Our response to God's Word is the key to the power of the Holy Scriptures!

When you hear God's Word, see God's Word and then take the most important step by responding to God's Word, you will be in one accord with God Himself. God is His Word. And God's Word is God. Turn over to the Book of John.

In the beginning was the Word, and the Word was with God, and the Word was God.

John 1:1 (NASB)

I cannot make it any simpler than this.

When God's Word is sown in you, and you respond positively to it, you are responding positively to God Himself. It's all about the Word, people!

Sometimes I just tear up and cry when I type this good stuff. I don't want you to read a book about me and see what I have done or how I get through a situation. I want you to *respond to the Word of God!* My book is just my testimony, my story of how I responded to God's Word. I write it not to become famous or wealthy. I don't need those things. I don't want those things! I already have God. I have El Shaddai, the God Who Is Enough! I lack for nothing! I write to show you and help you and hopefully inspire you to dig deep and seek Him with everything that is in you. I want you to respond to Him!

Remember Ruth? She cleansed herself. She anointed herself. She put on new clothes. She was commanded by Naomi to "prepare herself." Ruth was obedient. Part of that preparation was to be positioned at the feet of her kinsman redeemer. But don't forget the "big," "huge" part. She waited for Boaz to respond to her positioning and when he did, she "responded" back to him.

When you respond to God's Word (the seed), the power of God will work in your favor. When you position yourself, when you prepare yourself, you are making your will less and God's Will more. You are making yourself ready for what God has for you. It is no longer about you but all about God. Remember how the Mark 4:8 verse said, "they yielded a crop and produced thirty, sixty, and a hundredfold?"

Yielding is also huge. Huge! To yield is to produce or provide a crop or product. It also means "to give way." When you yield to the Word of God, you yield to God Himself. When you yield your ways, you "produce" God's Way. You give over and surrender or relinquish control to God.

Now let's walk out thirty, sixty, and a hundredfold. These are measures, or amounts, of fruit. These amounts of fruit can be measured by your response to God's Word in you. How do I know? I read His book! Are you not paying attention, people?

"If anyone has ears to hear, let him hear." And he was saying to them, "Take care what you listen to. By your standard of measure, it will be measured to you; and more will be given you besides. For whoever has, to him more shall be given; and whoever does not have even what he has shall be taken away from him."

Mark 4:23-25

The Hebrew phrase "if anyone has ears to hear, let him hear" also demands a response. Jesus warns them about who they listen to. He is saying that whoever listens to God, responds to God, and responds to God's Word. That person's measurement of response to God is the measurement God responds to that person and then some. Meaning God will always respond with more toward the person than the person toward God.

But, He also says that whoever listens to God and responds less or responds not at all, that person's measurement of response to God is the measurement God responds to that person, meaning that what he has is taken away.

This is a spiritual truth.

- Respond to God's Word.
- Accept God's Word.
- Put God's Word in you.

- Grow in God's Word.
- Grow to maturity in God's Word.
- When you mature in God's Word, you will produce fruit.
- Your fruit is harvested.
- Your harvest can be measured.
- Your fruit has seeds for future crops.
- The future crops you produce are for the Kingdom of God.

The more you respond to God the more God responds to you "and more will be given you besides."

Looking back, this season of purposeful handfuls starts out small and then gets larger. God allows my circumstances to stretch me and grow me. God's Word and my response to His Word make all the difference. God is about to stretch and grow me some more. I trust Him with everything...ok...not everything...but almost everything. Behold, people! God is up to something good!

He began to teach again by the sea. And such a very large crowd gathered to Him that He got into a boat in the sea and sat down; and the whole crowd was by the sea on the land. And he was teaching them many things in parables, and was saying to them in His teachings.

"Listen to this! Behold, the sower went out to sow; as he was sowing, some seed fell beside the road, and the birds came and ate it up.

Other seed fell on the rocky ground where it did not have much soil; and immediately it sprang up because it had no depth of soil. And after the sun had risen, it was scorched; and because it had no root, it withered away.

Other seed fell among the thorns, and the thorns came up and choked it, and it yielded no crop.

Other seeds fell into the good soil, and as they grew up and increased, they yielded a crop and produced thirty, sixty, and a hundredfold."

And He was saying, "He who has ears to hear, let him hear." As soon as He was alone, His followers, along with the twelve, began asking Him about the parables. And He was saying to them, "To you has been given the mystery of the Kingdom of God, but those who are outside get everything in parables, so that while seeing, they may see and not perceive, and while hearing, they may hear and not understand, otherwise they might return and be forgiven." And He said to them, "Do you not understand this parable? How will you understand all the parables?

The sower sows the word.

These are the ones who are beside the road where the word is sown; and when they hear, immediately Satan comes and takes away the word which has been sown in them.

In a similar way these are the ones on whom seed was sown on the rocky places, who, when they hear the word, immediately receive it with joy; and they have no firm root in themselves, but are only temporary; then, when affliction or persecution arises because of the word, immediately they fall away.

And others are the ones on whom seed was sown among the thorns, these are the ones who have heard the word, but the worries of the world, and the deceitfulness of riches, and the desires for other things enter in and choke the word, and it becomes unfruitful.

And those are the ones on whom seed was sown on the good soil; and they hear the word and accept it and bear fruit, thirty, sixty, and a hundredfold."

Mark 4:1-20 (NASB)

The Gospel

The Gospel is the teaching or revelation of Jesus Christ. It is often called the Good News. I like how Rabbi Baruch describes it as being the Good News concerning redemption.

Redemption is the action of saving or being saved from sin. It is a payment by Jesus Christ who died on the cross for our sins. He paid the price for our sin. His blood is the atonement for sin.

Redemption is, therefore, an outcome of Jesus. Did you know that Jesus means "salvation?"

Salvation is the deliverance from sin and its consequences, brought about by faith in Christ.

The first chapter of the Book of Mark starts out by proclaiming and declaring Jesus is the Son of God. He (Mark) backs it up by quoting from the Old Testament. More specifically from Isaiah.

The beginning of the gospel of Jesus Christ, the Son of God, as it is written in Isaiah the prophet: "Behold, I send My Messenger ahead of You, who will prepare Your way; the voice of one crying in the wilderness, make ready the way of the LORD, make His paths straight."

Mark 1:1-3 (NASB)

John was chosen by God Himself to be the first one to recognize the Messiah, Jesus Christ Himself. In fact, he was not even out of his mother Elizabeth's womb when they first met. He was about six-months along in her womb.

And behold, even your relative Elizabeth has also conceived a son in her old age; and she who was called barren is now in her sixth month. For nothing will be impossible with God.

Luke 1:36-37 (NASB)

When Elizabeth heard Mary's greeting, the baby leaped in her womb; and Elizabeth was filled with the Holy Spirit, and she cried out with a loud voice and said, "Blessed are you among women, and blessed is the fruit of your womb!"

Luke 1:41-42 (NASB)

There is that "fruit" again. If you want to be more like Jesus, then you have to have "fruit!"

John was called John the Baptist because he immersed people in the water to wash away their sins. John did not care for the things of this world. He did not worry about what he ate or drank. He did not worry about what he wore. John was all about the spiritual world. He lived out in the wilderness. The wilderness represents a place where a person must depend on God. John depended on God. John preached repentance and forgiveness. All the people of Judea and all the people of Jerusalem recognized God in him, and they would come out to the desert to be baptized by John in the water of the Jordan River. John was very humble.

And he was preaching, and saying, "After me, One is coming who is mightier than I, and I am not fit to stoop down and untie the thong of His sandals. I baptize you with water; but He will baptize you with the Holy Spirit."

Mark 1:7-8 (NASB)

Jesus came from Nazareth in Galilee and was baptized by John in the Jordan. Before we go further, note the not so noticeable place that Jesus comes from, "Nazareth in Galilee."

"...But later on He shall make it glorious, by the way of the sea, on the other side of Jordan, Galilee of the Gentiles. The people who walk in darkness will see a great light; those who live in a dark land, the light will shine on them."

Isaiah 9:1-2 (NASB)

This verse testifies that Jesus will come by way of the Sea of Galilee.

Then a shoot will spring forth from the stem of Jesse. And a branch from his roots will bear fruit. The Spirit of the Lord will rest on Him, the spirit of wisdom and understanding, the spirit of counsel and strength, the spirit of knowledge and the fear of the LORD.

Isaiah 11:1-2 (NASB)

This verse testifies that the "root" or "stem" or "branch" comes from Jesse. It is a prophecy about Messiah. Jesus, our Messiah, grew up in a city called Nazareth. Nazareth comes from one of the Hebrew words for "branch." Oh, and don't miss the Holy Spirit landing on Him part. This is good stuff, people!

So like the Bible says early on in the first chapter of Mark, "In those days," the people were looking for Messiah. They wanted to be prepared for when He comes. Now returning to where we were in Mark. Jesus was baptized by John the Immerser.

Immediately coming up out of the water; He saw the heavens opening, and the Spirit like a dove descending upon Him; and a voice came out of the heavens: "You are My beloved Son, in You I am well-pleased."

Mark 1:10-11 (NASB)

Jesus is baptized NOT because He was sinful or had any sin within Him, but because being baptized or immersed demonstrates His desire to submit to God and obey God's authority. Jesus is demonstrating that He is usable by God. This will glorify God. God the Father says, "In You I am well-pleased." In Hebrew, that means, "God deems Jesus to be righteous."

Jesus was not baptized because He was a sinner. God made sure that you know that Jesus was not a sinner by announcing to all that came out to the wilderness that this is His Son, and He is righteous!

Jesus was placed in the womb already having been conceived by the Holy Spirit. The Holy Child was placed in the womb of Mary. She was a surrogate mother to Jesus. Jesus did not have the DNA or sin-nature of Joseph from Joseph's sperm. He did not have the DNA or sin-nature of Mary from Mary's egg. He is sinless and therefore, perfect. God's DNA!

The dove that descended from heaven marks the end of a time-period. A new season has begun. The time of Jesus is now at hand. The last time a dove was used to signify the end of a time-period, was when Noah sent out the dove. The Lord had judged the land; the flood had come, marked by a new beginning when the dove did not return to the ark. John the Baptist's season of proclaiming the Lord was closing. He has been arrested.

Jesus immediately begins His new season by being impelled or cast by the Holy Spirit into the wilderness. He has been placed there to be dependent on God.

And He was in the wilderness forty days and being tempted by Satan; and He was with the wild beasts, and the angels were ministering to Him.

Mark 1:13 (NASB)

I like to keep my promises. In the chapter, I wrote named, "Ruth," I promised to talk about "lusts" later. Well, it is now later!

Lust shows up early in Scripture, all the way back in Genesis Chapter 3.

When the woman saw that the tree was good for food, and that it was a delight to the eyes, and that the tree was desirable to make one wise, she took from its fruit and ate; and she gave also to her husband with her and he ate.

Genesis 3:6 (NASB)

Eve fell for Satan's trickery. Remember he comes to steal, kill, and destroy. Satan can "trick" us. Satan attacks us by using "lust."

1. Lust of the eyes.
2. Lust of the flesh.
3. And lust of the boastful pride of life.

Eve failed because Eve relied on herself to engage with Satan. This is not going to be good, people!

Now forward to the Book of Matthew. Satan shows up to tempt, or trick, Jesus the way he did Eve. But Jesus is smarter than Satan. Satan attacks Jesus with "lust."

And the tempter (Satan) came and said to Him, "If You are the Son of God, command that these stones become bread."

Matthew 4:3 (NASB)

This is the lust of the flesh. Jesus was hungry. He has been in the wilderness.

But He answered and said, "It is written, 'Man shall not live by bread alone, but on every word that proceeds out of the mouth of God.'"

Matthew 4:4 (NASB)

Jesus-1. Satan-0. Jesus won because He fought with Scripture.

The devil took Him into the holy city and had Him stand on the pinnacle of the temple, and said to Him, "If You are the Son of God, throw Yourself down; for it is written, 'He will command His angels concerning you; and on their hands they will bear You up, so that You will not strike Your foot against a stone.'"

Matthew 4:5-6 (NASB)

This is the lust of the eyes. Satan wanted to win one. He tried to trick Jesus with Scripture right out of Psalm 91.

Jesus said to him, "On the other hand, it is written, 'You shall not put the LORD Your God to the test.'"

Matthew 4:7 (NASB)

Bam! Jesus-2. Satan-0. Jesus knows and intimately understands God's Word.

Again, the devil took Him to a very high mountain and showed Him all the kingdoms of the world and their glory; and he said to Him, "All these things I will give You, if You fall down and worship me."

Matthew 4:8-9 (NASB)

This is the lust of the boastful pride of life. Satan's third way to trick Jesus.

Then Jesus said to him, "Go, Satan! For it is written, 'You shall worship the LORD Your God, and serve Him only.'" The devil left Him; and behold, angels came and began to minister to Him.

Matthew 4:10-11 (NASB)

Jesus-3. Satan-0. This is good stuff, people! Jesus will always win! But, don't be fooled, you should not take on the enemy of your soul without Him!

The third place that "lust" shows up is in the Book of First John. Remember that three means verification in Hebrew. Verification is the process of establishing the truth, accuracy, or validity of something.

Do not love the world nor the things in the world. If anyone loves the world, the love of the Father is not in him. For all that is in the world, the lust of the flesh and the lust of the eyes and the boastful pride of life, is not from the Father, but is from the world. The world is passing away, and so also its lust; but the one who does the will of God lives forever.

1 John 2:15-17 (NASB)

The first time lusts are mentioned, Eve makes a classic mistake. Sin is committed and consequences are handed out. The second time lusts are mentioned, Jesus makes a classic win. Sin is not committed, and Jesus is victorious over the enemy of your soul. The third time lusts are mentioned, God warns us what will happen if we do not listen to Him. Sin will be committed, and consequences will be handed out. God warns us not to follow

43

Satan who is the temporary king of this world of flesh. That is why we need Jesus. He can conquer the sin of this world! And Satan too!

Coming back once again to the Book of Mark, chapter one. Jesus returns from the wilderness, and He comes to Galilee preaching the Gospel of God.

And saying (John the Baptist), "The time is fulfilled, and the kingdom of God is at hand; repent and believe in the gospel."

Mark 1:15 (NASB)

It's important to note "repent" and "believe" in that order.

A non-believer can repent and turn from their way to God's way, thus leading to "belief" in God which leads to "faith" in God. You can't have faith in God without the first step of repentance (recognizing who you are compared to God, meaning you are unholy, and He is Holy). Repentance means that you respond to God by turning from your own way to His way. You submit to His authority, and you believe (commit) to Him by taking a step of faith. Faith leads to obedience.

As He was going along by the Sea of Galilee, He saw Simon (Peter) and Andrew, the brother of Simon, casting a net in the sea; for they were fishermen.

Mark 1:16 (NASB)

Jesus is in Galilee, which is very important because Jesus, the Messiah, was to come from Galilee. The Messiah is to come from Galilee. The people are watching for Him in Galilee.

The people who walk in darkness will see a great light; those who live in a dark land, the light will shine on them.

Isaiah 9:2 (NASB)

God is light, and in Him, there is no darkness at all.

1 John 1:5 (NASB)

Jesus (God in flesh form), the Messiah, is the Light of the World.

And Jesus said to them, "Follow Me, and I will make you fishers of men."

Mark 1:17 (NASB)

Jesus said "come after Me" and I will make you fish for men.

Immediately they left their nets and followed Him.

Mark 1:18 (NASB)

Simon Peter and Andrew (brothers) left their nets (repented and turned from what they were doing, turned from their own ways), and then followed Him (believed in, had faith in, obeyed Him).

Going on a little farther, He saw James the son of Zebedee and John his brother, who were also in the boat mending the nets. Immediately He called them; and they left their father Zebedee in the boat with the hired servants, and went away to follow Him.

Mark 1:19-20 (NASB)

Jesus, going on, but still in Galilee, sees two more brothers: James and John. He calls them and they respond to Him. They repent and turn from their way, their old way, and they follow Him.

Why would two sets of brothers drop what they are doing and follow a man they have just been called to on the Sea of Galilee? In Hebrew, two is the number of "witness." The number two bears witness.

They dropped what they were doing because the brothers knew their Scripture! They were Jewish brothers who knew the Jewish Scripture! We call it the Old Testament. Some people don't like to study the Old Testament because they do not believe it applies to them because the church has the "New Covenant." Well, to quote the French Peas in the Veggie Tale movies, "You silly little pickles!"

The Old Testament confirms and affirms the New Testament and vice versa. They witness to one another over and over and over again. Turn to Genesis 48. This is good stuff, people! Genesis 48 has Jacob blessing the two sons of Joseph (Ephraim and Manasseh are brothers). Did you catch that? Brothers. Jacob is speaking.

The angel who has redeemed me from all evil, bless the lads; and may my name live on in them, and the names of my fathers Abraham and Isaac; and may they grow into a multitude in the midst of the earth.

Genesis 48:16 (NASB)

This passage is known to the Jewish people as "The Blessing of Messiah."

The angel (translated the servant of God) **who has redeemed** (only Messiah can redeem, meaning buy you back from your sins, make a payment for your sins) **me from all evil** (sin)**, bless the lads** (young men)**, and may my name** (Jacob) **live on in them, and the names of my fathers Abraham and Isaac** (whenever you see the patriarchs' names think of blessings and the promises of God)**; and may they grow into a multitude in the midst of the earth** (land)**.**

Yup, you missed it! For years, I missed it too! Look again! Read this last passage again. Then read on.

Focus on the word "grow." My Bible is a NASB which says "grow." It has the Hebrew word "1711" next to it. If you turn to the Hebrew 1711 in the back of the book it says, "dag-gaw" meaning to move rapidly; become numerous; grow.

The problem is that it was translated and marked 1711. WRONG! Look in a Hebrew Bible.

It is actually "dag-gaw," but 1710, meaning...wait for it... "Fish."

So this is the best part! The end of the verse in Mark says, "May they fish into a multitude (mankind) in the midst of the earth (land)."

They, the young men, blessed brothers will become... "Fishers (fisherman) of fish (men) on land" which is their new way and no longer "fishers of fish in the water" which is their old way. Ugh! This is so cool!

The brothers Simon and Andrew and brothers, James and John, knew their Hebrew Scripture. They, along with everyone else, knew that the Messiah would be revealed in Galilee. They knew that Messiah would call young men who, through the promises and blessings of the Patriarchs Abraham, Isaac, and Jacob, would be called to "fish on land," or the more familiar term, "fish for men on land." Ugh again! I just love this stuff!

Looking back, I know you are getting tired of all of this Scripture. Don't hold your breath for an apology from me. You will turn blue and die first. I hope you have Jesus! I share each step in Scripture because it is important for you to see and read and hear and know God's Word. Not my opinion. Not my "ideas." I want you to be able to go and grow verse by verse, too.

I want you to recognize the reoccurring themes of Ruth, a Kinsman-Redeemer, and changing from pleasant to bitter and then back to pleasant (a new pleasant, one in her lap that brings hope and a future). There are other themes like thirty, sixty, and hundredfold and sowing God's Word, the seed, into the fields (the world) so that at harvest time the believers can be gathered up. The seed is God's Word and seed can make bread. The Word of God is the Bread of Life! The seed can be called fruit. Fruit is important. The Light of the World needs to be taken into the dark corners of this world. Obedience and willingness to respond to God are also important themes. God is growing us and changing us to be more like Him. I love every bit of this stuff! God is consistent, people! You will see how all of this comes into play in the coming chapters as God stretches and begins to grow me in new ways. May you repent and believe, and obey His call in your life to become "fishers of men!"

Time To Be Stretched

It is the fall of the year 2006. Our church has opened its door to the enemy of our soul and to missionaries that share the Gospel. Both. Our church has its annual mission's week. We celebrate missionaries that visit our church. We build relationships with them, and they share about their relationships with the people groups that they serve. This morning we have a special missionary visiting our Sunday School Class. I slide into the back row seat. Old habits die hard. I do that in case I get paged to the preschool or children's area. It does happen. Lots of times, I am not paged by phone or by a device but by the fire alarm that a preschooler has pulled because it is pretty and red (and mom or dad was not looking).

The missionary is from "Kmart." (For security reasons, I cannot name the country.) He knows John, the musician. John spent a couple of years in "Kmart." The missionary is telling us about his mission field. His field turns out not to be in "Kmart." "Kmart" is just the staging country for his real ministry which is in "Target." (For security reasons, I cannot name this closed country.) Persians? Is he a Persian missionary? Wow. I perk up. I've never met another Persian believer or a missionary to Persia. This is exciting. God has already been stretching me to minister to the people of Persia. My people. Right now, I like the Jewish people better. Can't I just go back to Israel? Ugh.

So, I listen. The missionary speaks of places and people that are familiar to me. I have not been around anything Persian other than my dad since 1993. Do Persian cats count? It's 2006, and I am feeling homesick. He speaks, and I drift off. Kabuli palau (rice with raisins and carrots), bulanis (spicy meat and vegetable pies), roht (traveling sweet bread), and halwa (Afghan sweet) begin to float around in my memory which makes my mouth water and my tummy growl.

I sit up and hope that the lady next to me did not hear that. The kids are away on their weekend visitation, and I was alone this morning, so I slept in and skipped breakfast. Tea, I love Persian tea. If done right, there is a bit of spice to it. Sugar cubes or sugar hard candy disks that you slip on your tongue to sugar your tea when it pours over the sweet treat in your mouth. Tea is served in little cups. Well, actually glasses. Oops, off on a bunny trail again. Sorry.

I tune in to hear him say that he wants to gather up a group of people from this church to go on a mission trip to "Kmart." They would go through "Kmart" and go into "Target." The group would prayer walk and look like tourists. However, secretly, our mission would be to bring Persian Bibles into "Target." Wait, what? Isn't that dangerous?

He then says, "This is a pretty dangerous mission trip." Ok. I'm out. No way! Not me. No stretchy-stretchy, Lord. Not this time. But I keep listening. He goes on to tell about areas that other groups have gone into prayer walk. They have had great breakthroughs with salvations and secret churches starting. I try to return to the subject of food. Don't listen, Shahe! Think of those wonderful Afghan parties and the naan (bread) dipped into korma (spicy stew beef). I am getting hungry again.

He then says, "The people are very hungry for the Word of God. The Word of God is the Bread of Life." Wait, what? Is this man in my head? Get out! No way! Not me. No stretching me Lord! Not this time. Can't I just go back to Israel? It's only dangerous at the airport; the rest is a piece of cake. I like cake.

He then says, "The Persian people are poor physically and spiritually. They have bread, but they are hungry for cake. They have Islam, and some have Zoroastrianism, but they want more." Wait, what? No! No! No! I am not going to do this. I shut him down. Yes, him the missionary, but also HIM the God Who created me, and right now, He is totally messing with me.

I love you, Lord, with my everything...well...evidently almost everything...but this is too much. They arrest people for this kind of stuff. They lock people up! There is no Kabuli Palau and roht in prison. They kill people like me. Did you forget? I used to be one of them. They don't like people that convert. They don't like

people that get divorced. They don't like people that like Jews and
Israel. Hello up there! Are you listening to me? No!

I am sitting with my arms crossed and over my chest. Nothing is getting into my heart. My body language is not speaking Persian right now. It is speaking, "I have just shut down the God of the Universe and built a huge wall with one breath and a pout for good measure."

I tune in to hear him ask if anyone has any questions. He just stands there. Nope. No questions. Time to go, people! But he stands there. And he waits for a question. Ugh! So I sit there pouting and think to myself, the only question I have is that I wonder if he has a Persian Bible with him. I have never seen one or put my hands on it. I would like to do that. But I never speak up.

Again, he asks if anyone has any questions. Nothing. No one. The man just waits. What's up with that? Let's get on with this. Yes, I would like to know if you have a Persian Bible with you, but I'm not going to ask you because, if I do, you will answer. And if you answer, "Yes," then I am going to want to see it and touch it, and I just know my walls will start to break. It only takes a touch. I am a pile of mush. I am not going to raise my hand and ask. No way! This pile of mush was trying to prove she had a backbone. Where is a disobedient toddler with a fire alarm habit when you need him?

The poor man finally asks a third time, and the girl next to me raises her hand. She asks, "Do you have a Persian Bible with you?" Wait, what? Before I can sit up and unlock my clenched arms, the missionary dude is reaching past several rows to hand her a Persian Bible. She thumbs it and hands it to me. Wait, what? Get that away from me; I don't want to touch it. It's as if the book had boy cooties and I was in the first-grade. I pull back, but she places the book in my hands. Ugh.

Down comes the wall I just built. Up come the tears I am just now forming. In my hands is a most powerful book. Not because it is written in Persian but because God wrote it. I am a pile of mush with no backbone and unable to move.

The class finally adjourns, I place the book with the cooties on the table by the missionary who asks too many questions, and I bolt from the room. No way, God! No way! I am out of there!

I head to the Preschool Welcome Desk. Do you need me? Nope. Everything is calm and fully staffed. I head up to the Children's Welcome Desk. Before I can ask do you need me, Mr. Bob goes on and on how smooth everything is this morning. All is well. Well, I guess I can go on to service then. And I head off to the back of the worship center.

I sit down in one of my favorite back row pews. Can't get to me back here, I think. Our pastor is not speaking. It's another man, but I missed his introduction. He starts by saying, "I bet you expect me to start in Matthew 28 and speak about the Great Commission. I want you to turn to Genesis Chapter 12." Wait, what? Not again. Lord, give me a break.

I know Chapter 12 of Genesis. I am very familiar with it. I don't need to turn there. This is the chapter that God used to break me and make me new with my attitude toward the Jewish people and the nation of Israel. Seriously, this is not funny God!

He goes on. Here are his highlights.

- Once God reveals something to you, you become responsible for it.
- When God reveals the Great Commission to you, you need to be obedient and to go and make disciples of all nations.
- Genesis Chapter 12, Abram is from Ur. God says, "Just go."
- Abram obeys and through a series of obedient responses to God, the seed of Abraham is established, and blessings occur.
- Genesis 18:18, "Since Abraham will surely become a great and mighty nation, and in him all the nations of the earth will be blessed."
- Genesis 22:18, "In your seed all the nations of the earth shall be blessed because you have obeyed My voice."

- Psalm 22:27-28, "All the ends of the earth will remember and turn to the LORD, and all the families of the nations will worship before You. For the kingdom is the LORD's and He rules over the nations."

Bet you are wondering about now how I have all of these Scriptures in order? Well, I wrote them down. I wrote them down kicking and screaming; but, buddy, I wrote them. I may not agree with them right about now, and I don't want to hear more; but, I write them down.

- Psalm 59:9, "Because of his strength I will watch for You for God is my stronghold."
- Psalm 67, "God be gracious to us and bless us, and cause His face to shine upon us-that Your way may be known on earth, Your salvation among all nations. Let the peoples praise You, O God; let all the peoples praise You. Let the nations be glad and sing for joy; for You will judge the peoples with uprightness and guide the nations on the earth. Let the peoples praise You, O God; let all the peoples praise You. The earth has yielded its produce; God, our God, blesses us. God blesses us. That all the ends of the earth may fear Him."

Really? I like the number 67. I was born in 1967. This is a Psalm about the salvation of Israel. I know that. Can't I just go to Israel? I like it there! They like me. Well, most of them like me, except security personnel, but everyone else does.

- Psalm 88:9, "All nations whom You have made shall come and worship before You, O Lord, and they shall glorify Your name."
- Psalm 96:1-3, "Sing to the LORD a new song; sing to the LORD, all the earth. Sing to the LORD, bless His name; proclaim good tidings of His salvation from day to day. Tell of His glory among the nations, His wonderful deeds among all the peoples."

I am cracking and arguing at the same time. How can this man know? How can I go? I can't go, Lord! Surely, You are not sending me to "Target?"

- Isaiah 6:7-8, "He touched my mouth with it and said, "Behold, this has touched your lips; and your iniquity is taken away and your sin is forgiven." Then I heard the voice of the Lord saying, "Whom shall I send, and who will go for Us?" Then I said, "Here am I. Send me!"

Aw, come on now! This is not fair. It's three against one. (Just in case you did not get that, it is God the Father, God the Son, and God the Holy Spirit against little old me.) Little old mush of me who is melting to my knees between the pews. I'm going down, people!

- Isaiah 49:6, "He says, 'It is too small a thing that You should be My Servant to raise up the tribes of Jacob and to restore the preserved ones of Israel; I will also make You a light to the nations so that My salvation may reach to the end of the earth.'"
- Matthew 24:14, "This gospel of the kingdom shall be preached in the whole world as a testimony to all the nations, and then the end will come."
- Mark 13:10, "The gospel must first be preached to all the nations."
- Luke 24:46-47, "and He said to them, 'Thus it is written, that the Christ would suffer and rise again from the dead the third day, and that repentance for forgiveness of sins would be proclaimed in His name to all the nations, beginning from Jerusalem.'"

What is this, Bible Drill? It's hard to write when your vision is blurred. I suddenly feel more like the bitter woman Mara than the pleasant one Naomi. I can only see my circumstances with my flesh eyes, and I am scared, and it's getting hard not to sob in public. My nose is running, and I have no tissues. I am a mess on the floor of the church, thanking God no one is sitting behind me watching me wipe my nose on my sweater.

- Acts 1:8, "But you will receive power when the Holy Spirit has come upon you; and you shall be My witnesses both in Jerusalem, and in all Judea and Samaria, and even to the remotest part of the earth."
- Romans 10:13-15, "For 'Whoever will call on the name of the LORD will be saved.' How then will they call on Him in whom they have not believed? How will they believe in Him whom they have not heard? And how will they hear without a preacher? How will they preach unless they are sent? Just as it is written, 'How beautiful are the feet of those who bring good news of good things!'"
- 2 Corinthians 5:18-20, "Now all things are from God, who reconciled us to Himself through Christ and gave us the ministry of reconciliation, namely, that God was in Christ reconciling the world to Himself, not counting their trespasses against them, and He has committed to us the word of reconciliation. Therefore, we are ambassadors for Christ, as though God were making an appeal through us; we beg you on behalf of Christ, be reconciled to God."

Forget it; I am crying ugly all over again as I type this. These words still get me. The sequence still gets me. The words get me from my place of resistance to a place of reconciliation.

But back to the pile of the mess who is me on the floor of the church. I find myself telling God, "Here I am, send me." I find myself apologizing in prayer to all the other hundreds of people in this room that endured a Bible Drill lesson while God used a missionary man who gave little of his opinion from the pulpit but allowed God to speak Scripture to me over and over and over again. You see, I have a big wall to come down. Huge! It will take more than one hit from a wrecking ball. It will take a lot of hits to wreck my resistance and break down my wall so that God can start building up something new. This man went on and on.

- Galatians 3:8, "The Scripture, foreseeing that God would justify the Gentiles by faith, preached the gospel beforehand to Abraham, saying, 'All the nations will be blessed in you.'"

- Revelation 21:22-24, "I saw no temple in it, for the Lord God the Almighty and the Lamb are its temple. And the city has no need of the sun or of the moon to shine on it, for the glory of God has illuminated it, and its lamp is the Lamb. The nations will walk by its light, and the kings of the earth will bring their glory into it."
- Revelation 22:1-2, "Then he showed me a river of the water of life, clear as crystal, coming from the throne of God and of the Lamb, in the middle of its street. On either side of the river was the tree of life, bearing twelve kinds of fruit, yielding its fruit every month; and the leaves of the tree were for the healing of the nations."

Now God is just showing off.

- The man goes on to say that the word nations appears over 800 times in the Bible. Grace appears over 170 times. Salvation appears over 160 times. Love appears over 300 times.
- He is the light to our path. The love of God. The passion of God. All authority of heaven and earth is with you.
- Integrity. Why integrity? Because, you need to do what Jesus says to do.
- Revelation 15:4, "Who will not fear, O Lord, and glorify Your name? For You alone are holy; for all the nations will come and worship before you, for Your righteous acts have been revealed."
- He says that you have closeness to God when He asks to whom shall I send and you respond, "Here I am, send me."
- You can never be fully obedient until God's passion is your own.
- Revelation 7:9-10, "After these things I looked, and behold, a great multitude which no one could count, from every nation, and all tribes and peoples and tongues, standing before the throne and before the Lamb clothed in white robes, and palm branches were in their hands; and they cry out with a loud voice, saying, 'Salvation to our God who sits on the throne, and to the Lamb.'"

- The task is clear and in focus. The kingdom of God will grow if you are faithful to the task.

Oh, this guy is good. And yes, Jesus is too! He continues.

1. You have to have a love of God and be passionate about the nations.
2. The purpose is salvation, not for our benefit but to share it.
3. You are responsible for the gospel.
4. No people group is outside of the love of God; the scope is compassion.
5. You will get special instructions from God.
6. Focus on Scripture about the nations.
7. The key to purpose lies with our relationship to God. It is a passionate pursuit if you want to find your true purpose.
8. Daily humility and confession to Him.
9. It is God's mission, His.
10. There is a 10-40 window. 2 billion people. 2200 people groups. He is the Lord of the Harvest.

He then closes with Luke 1:37, "For with God, nothing is impossible."

It is November 15th, 2006. How do I know? Because, I wrote it in my Bible. The Redeemer Banner is on the stage. I am on the floor. I am going to the country of "Target" in the spring of 2007.

Looking back, I can see the wrecking ball swinging and a direct hit with every verse of Scripture. I can't believe I have them all and that I wrote down his whole speech. I rarely, if ever, do that. But God knew that I would need to refer to them again and again, especially when I took my eyes off of Him and began to get scared. These verses gave me a hope and a future and let me know that God's plan was for me to say, "Here I am, send me." Did I know if I would come back safe? No. I didn't ask that. That part was not important anymore. What was important was that I surrendered my will for His Will. His will was for me to go. If you are in God's Will, then you are in the safest place you can be.

Before writing, I prayed about what I was going to write. As I read my Bible, I picked up my blue one. It is tattered and torn. It has a broken binding and pages are ripped from searching sessions. I have dragged this book around the world and back again. But the really neat gift is that I wrote in it.

I wrote when I studied Ruth, and I wrote the information about Mark chapter four. I can tell you where God showed me to go to Israel in 2005 and where He did it again in 2006. I can show you the long list of verses that I call my "wrecking ball verses" that convince a timid and afraid daughter of the Most High God that she should go to a place that would not welcome her.

I usually end a chapter with the verses that I write about, but this time, I have put the verses in the chapter. I will leave you with this one. I wrote it across the page from my "wrecking ball verses."

Figure out what will please Christ, and then do it.

Ephesians 5:8-10 (The Message)

I encourage you to read all of Ephesians Chapter 5 in the Message. This is good stuff, people!

Watch what God does, and then you do it, like children who learn proper behavior from their parents. Mostly what God does is love you. Keep company with him and learn a life of love. Observe how Christ loved us. His love was not cautious but extravagant. He didn't love in order to get something from us but to give everything of himself to us. Love like that.

Don't allow love to turn into lust, setting off a downhill slide into sexual promiscuity, filthy practices, or bullying greed. Though some tongues just love the taste of gossip, Christians have better uses for language than that. Don't talk dirty or silly. That kind of talk doesn't fit our style. Thanksgiving is our dialect.

You can be sure that using people of religion or things just for what you can get out of them-the usual variations on idolatry-will get you nowhere, and certainly nowhere near the kingdom of Christ, the kingdom of God.

Don't let yourselves get taken in by religious smooth talk. God gets furious with people who are full of religious sales talk but want nothing to do with him. Don't even hang around people like that.

You groped your way through that murk once, but no longer. You're out in the open now. The bright light of Christ makes your way plain. So no more stumbling around. Get on with it! The good, the right, the true-these are the actions appropriate for daylight hours. Figure out what will please Christ, and then do it.

Don't waste your time on useless work, mere busywork, the barren pursuits of darkness. Expose these things for the sham they are. It's a scandal when people waste their lives on things they must do in the darkness where no one will see. Rip the cover off those frauds and see how attractive they look in the light of Christ.

Wake up from your sleep, climb out of your coffins; Christ will show you the light!

So watch your step. Use your head. Make the most of every chance you get. These are desperate times! Don't live carelessly, unthinkingly. Make sure you understand what the Master wants.

Don't drink too much wine. That cheapens your life. Drink the Spirit of God, huge draughts of him. Sing hymns instead of drinking songs! Sing songs from your heart to Christ. Sing praises over everything, any excuse for a song to God the Father in the name of our Master, Jesus Christ.

Ephesians 5:1-20 (The Message)

Going

I am going to "Target." Great. Thanks a lot, God. I guess to be more accurate; I am going to "Target" kicking, screaming, and whining to God. I would love to type that I immediately responded to God with great enthusiasm and with joy...does that make me look a bit like "rocky ground" to you? I tried to resist.

But I will admit that I fail. I don't always respond to God with great enthusiasm and joy but with fear and dread. Are you sure God? Really? Why me? Can't I just go back to Israel? Do I have to witness to Persians? Do I have to share the gospel with Muslims? Why do I have to be obedient? Why can't I just be me and, well, kick, and scream, and whine? It's when I get to the end of my dumb responses that I just...respond. "Ok." "Here I am, send me."

There is nothing wrong with being honest with God and with others about your relationship with God. Do you remember the child's song, "I'm gonna let it shine?" The song is from Mark chapter 4 and yes, here we go again. Sorry. Well, not really. I'm still going to share more verses.

And He (Jesus) was saying to them, "A lamp is not brought to be put under a basket, is it, or under a bed? Is it not brought to be put on the lampstand?"

Mark 4:21 (NASB)

This means that Jesus wants us to shine Him and put Him (the Light of the World) out in the open (like on a lampstand) for everyone to see and experience the light that shines. His light!

So I go home after church. I take my sermon notes that I wrote and rewrote them on the inside of my blue Bible. This is necessary because I have tears and probably snot on the pages and I want to be able to read what I've written down.

I return to the church tired. I am praying for provision. I spout off a prayer/need. Or is that need in a prayer? But I say,

"Lord I guess if you are going to send me then you will have to provide a way for me to go financially." It was short and simple.

Monday morning rolls around. I am at work, and I get a call. It's a local church, and they want to know if I do murals for preschool and children's areas. "Why, yes," I reply. They ask, "Can you come and see our church and give us your ideas and what you would do with the space?" Sure! They might not have been ready to hire me, but I knew I had the job. They might not have been ready for me, but God provided them. I make plans to meet with them.

The following Sunday, Rabbi Baruch is in town. He is traveling through from one speaking engagement to another in the states. I always make it a point to go and listen because God always reveals Himself to me in new ways through direct teaching from the Word of God. He just uses Rabbi Baruch. Never "follow" a man or a "man who teaches." Follow the Lord God Almighty's teachings through men of integrity in the Word of God.

It begins and I wonder if he will share a word that will confirm that I am going to "Target." Now, pause a minute. Seriously, I am such a weakling! I have had a Sunday full of confirmation after confirmation to go on this mission trip to "Target." He has given me verse after verse of assurance in Scripture. I just know, without a shadow of a doubt, that He is even going to provide for the trip financially by painting in a church and yet...I sit here wanting "more." More, really? Oh me of little faith. I repent, and I sit quietly.

Rabbi Baruch starts to teach and once again, having a man read the Hebrew right out of a Hebrew Bible just blows my Ruth socks off. He is talking about obedience and when God commands...what is our response? Ugh. He ends this time with an invitation to come to Israel. But it was the way God lead him to say it; I can't even put it into words because he was speaking but God was piercing my heart..."You are going back to Israel Shahe." Wait, what?

Rabbi Baruch says, "Amen." Our time is ended but wait, what? I'm not done yet. *Lord, did I hear you right? Am I going back to Israel in fall of 2007?* I smart off. Ok, I'm honest. I did smart off to God. *"Well, I guess You will have to provide another church for me to paint!"* Like that will happen I smirk. I can be such a stiff-necked Orpah.

Monday morning rolls around. I am at work, and I get a call. It's a local church, and they want to know if I do murals for preschool and children's areas. "Why, yes," I reply. They ask, "Can you come and see our church and give us your ideas and what you would do with the space?" Sure! They might not have been ready to hire me, but I knew I had the job. They might not have been ready for me, but God provided them. I make plans to meet with them.

Did you notice that the above paragraph is a complete repeat? Well, it is. And I did it because God repeated and knocked me over and out of my Ruth socks again. Two trips in 2007. One in the fall and one in the spring. Two Churches to paint. One in the winter and one in the summer. Wow! God is amazing! I am not amazing. I am just amazed…at Him.

Looking back, I responded. God responded too. I responded again. God responded again. God and I have a real relationship. He is my God, and I am His child. He is my Husband, and I am the Bride of Christ. He has a plan, and I plan to get on board His plan. It's got a hope and a future you know!

Besides it's hard not to increase in faith when you see God increase more in you.

I choose humility which leads to hearing God more. Hearing God more leads to knowing God's Will and God's Way. Knowing God's Will and God's Way leads me to submit to the authority of God. Submission to God's authority brings rewards from God. Rewards from God increase my trust and faith in God. Increasing my faith and trust in God leads me to the calming of my soul. The calming of my soul, allows me to rest in Him. Resting in Him is wonderful!

I would rather depend on God than depend on myself. It's all about making choices!

"If anyone has ears to hear, let him hear." And he was saying to them, "Take care what you listen to. By your standard of measure, it will be measured to you; and more will be given you besides. For whoever has, to him more shall be given; and whoever does not have even what he has shall be taken away from him."

Mark 4:23-25 (NASB)

'For I know the plans that I have for you,' declares the LORD, 'plans for welfare and not for calamity to give you a future and a hope.'

Jeremiah 29:11 (NASB)

Three?

As Christmas approaches, church work has a small season of rest. For me and the area of the church that I work in, it is just after the preschool and children have their musical programs. It's just Sunday School and parties, and I love this time of year. Not because of Santa! Nope! That pagan is history. I love how prophecy is fulfilled by the Messiah. Rabbi Baruch says that "the spirit of prophecy is the testimony of Messiah."

So during this time, I have time off from church, and I have lots of time with my brown babies. They are growing up too fast! I love that their Christian school gives them lots of time off, and I love time with them. The hard part is that I have to share them for one week of the three weeks off. During that annual and dreaded time, I spend time praying, sometimes fasting, and studying my Bible.

Year after year, God uses this time, to "tell" me or "guide" me through His Word to what my next year will look like. In this case, the year 2007. While reading and studying, I get this overwhelming prompting by the Holy Spirit that I am taking three trips in 2007. Three? But "Target" and Israel make two? Yes, you silly little pickles, I am a bit on the slow side. I quote Veggie Tales, people! There is something seriously not right about me!

Three? Where? What is trip number three? There can't be three trips! I don't have time to paint three churches! Ugh! But again, time passes, and I get lead to my small file cabinet. I open it up to the folder "important papers." Sounds important, right? Well, it's where I put stuff that I know is important, but I don't know where else to file them.

I pull out a certificate and letter that I received after our trip in 2002 to Walt Disney World. It seems someone had filed and won a class-action lawsuit, and my vacation was on that list. For five years I have had this fifty-percent off certificate for a Walt Disney World vacation. Until this time we have not used it because…well, lack of money, people! It's expensive.

I tell you it's expensive, but I am also telling God the same thing. I look through the information and realize that it has a time limit and date limit. I knew it expired in 2007 but for some reason, because our trip was in August 2002, I thought it would expire in August 2007. It expires at the end of May 2007. Before summer vacation. Disney? Are we going back to Disney?

God showed me Disney, "Target," and then Israel. No way. My calendar said, "Target," Disney, Israel according to all the commitments that I had to work around.

The kids return from their week away. The New Year is rung in with us watching Disney movies and playing games. God wins His way. I get on board and try to plan for three trips. Ugh.

Looking back, I can see the hand of the Lord guiding me gently and with power. You can't make a vessel out of clay without both. I am mush in His hands. And I am ok with that.

The word which came to Jeremiah from the LORD saying, "Arise and go down to the potter's house, and there I will announce My words to you."

Then I went down to the potter's house, and there he was, making something on the wheel. But the vessel that he was making of clay was spoiled in the hand of the potter; so he remade it into another vessel, as it pleased the potter to make.

Then the word of the LORD came to me saying, "Can I not, O house of Israel, deal with you as this potter does?" declares the LORD. "Behold, like the clay in the potter's hand, so are you in My hand, O house of Israel."

Jeremiah 18:1-6 (NASB)

I call the Disney representative and work out details for a possible one week trip. We will drive down on a Saturday, stay at our one-hour away cheap hotel and then start Disney on Sunday. We will do the mouse proud from Sunday to Saturday and leave late that night to crash at our favorite cheap motel. We will drive back on Sunday.

My kids will miss a week of school. My kids always get perfect medals for perfect attendance each year. Seriously, they don't miss school. I am a single mom who would have to take time off from work to juggle sick kids, so I often pray for healthy kids and not to miss work. Be careful what you pray for, God will grant them if they are in His will. It's like my truck. It has over a hundred thousand miles on it right now. A white Chevy S-10 that I pray for to have few repairs and if they are needed to be inexpensive. I pray for safety in travel and safety for the truck when we are not in it. I pray a blessing over it the way I pray blessings over the kids. God answers prayers, people! I ask the kids if they are ok with not getting a medal this year, they respond with a YES!

I also enter into a new type of fast. God uses Isaiah 58 to lead me. For one week it was no food, just water. Then it changed. God talked to me about a fast of silence. He would allow me to talk if the conversation pertained to Him, my kids (parenting), or my church work. Nothing else. Silence. Well, if you have not figured it out yet, I can talk! If you give me a Coke Cola, I can talk really fast! So I explain to those around me, and I just get silent. I fast "silently" for forty days. It was hard to do, but it did show me how much of what came out of my mouth (which means it is in my heart) was good and about Him or not good and not about Him. It was an eye opening and mouth closing experience! It is also a great learning tool for the season ahead with my home church. "Talk" is going to begin to rip our church wide open, with Satan's help of course. What an angel!

I start painting at the "Hill Church." I changed the name for safety and security reasons. They like what I proposed and agreed to pay for my trip to Israel instead of a direct employee type of payment. It's a win-win for the church and me. They get a whole preschool painted in a Noah's Ark theme including hallways and classrooms. It also includes several canvas prints for each classroom of the children's favorite Bible stories. My trip to Israel paid.

Work is hard but if you are faithful to God…I know what you are expecting here…then God is faithful to you. But you are WRONG! God is always faithful! So I need to say it like this, God is faithful so I respond by being faithful in my work to complete it and do it to the best of my ability.

During this time I am also already meeting with the mission team that will be going to "Target." We are planning and praying and preparing for this trip. There are six of us going. Four girls and two guys. Our missionary contact will join us in "Kmart" which will make us seven, perfect! Did you catch that Hebrew number?

Looking back, one of the best parts of being a believer is prayer and prayers are amazing. So is unity. Put praying believers together in unity and you have a powerful force for the Kingdom of God. A cloud of witnesses! We have hope!

Therefore, since we have so great a cloud of witnesses surrounding us, let us also lay aside every encumbrance and the sin which so easily entangles us, and let us run with endurance the race that is set before us, fixing our eyes on Jesus the author and perfecter of faith, who for the joy set before Him endured the cross, despising the shame, and has sat down at the right hand of the throne of God.

Hebrews 12:1-2 (NASB)

First Prayer Update

We are committed to prayer for the trip. I send out the following email as my first email prayer request for the trip. I send a picture of a woman fully clothed in an Islamic Hijab.

I knew when I took this picture last spring 2006 in Israel that I would "go" somewhere to help someone just like this woman. She just sat there, hidden and faceless to the world except that one hand that was small and fragile looking. She was asking for money, and we gave her some. I remember walking away thinking, "God I wish I could do more, help me to learn how to do more." I have a second chance in the world; I'm no longer a Muslim lady who has no future. I have Christ Jesus who has given me freedom, forgiveness, mercy, love, joy and salvation, and He and He alone can give that precious gift. He alone offers me an eternal future. All I have to do is tell others and share His gift with them.

Trip Details. This is just an introduction email, to ask if you would be willing to commit praying for our team.

For the last two weeks, I have been praying over and gathering names that I felt like God wanted me to include. I have tried several times to start to send this email, but today was the day God said to send it. God had me choose 50 people. The number 50 is Jubilee and all debts are free, a celebration of incomplete and grace (the number 5) times completeness (the number 10).

I will be sending emails/updates and specific prayer requests to you.

We need people who will be willing to pray for our team of six. This is a serious request. Nothing as a team of our own ability is going to make this a successful one. Only prayer and God with the team member as the vessels will make this trip work. So when you commit to pray, please do pray. We will be in heavy spiritual warfare. We intend to take God's Word into a dark corner of the world that is desperate for illumination. The country is considered "closed" to missions and evangelism but in Luke, it says "Nothing is impossible with God." Luke 1:37. I believe with all my heart that if you are willing to join in this that there will be a blessing for you too. I believe that God is going to do something amazing. I believe that He has plans that will glorify Himself and that we as a team are going to have the privilege of participating if we are willing and able to set our own "stuff" aside. I believe that if we set aside our unbelief and recognize who He is in this process that He will reveal Himself in a mighty and powerful way. He is moving, and we just need to move in Him and with Him.

We call our destination country "Target." Our staging country (where we go before and after the "Target" country) is called "Kmart." I have verbally said where we are going to most of you but in my emails to you for prayer, the name of the country will not be mentioned for security reasons.

Prayer for today:

- Pray for our six team members.
- Pray for our team leader, as he makes the final arrangement with tickets, dates, and visas.
- Pray for our visas to be accepted and approved.
- Pray for our contact in "Kmart" to be able to make his preparations for us.
- Pray for our hearts to align with God and His will for what He wants for this trip.
- Pray that our expectations be that God is glorified and His will is done.
- Pray that we be satisfied with whatever comes our way, that we are flexible and willing to be a usable vessel.

Father, I pray that You renew a right spirit within me, a spirit not born of fear, or from self-sufficiency, or from an ungodly independence. Fill me with Your spirit of love and grace, as I rely upon You to restore to me the joy of Your salvation. Help me to be usable by You. In Jesus' Name, I pray, Amen.

I ended it with thanking my dear friends. No one that I asked to be a part of the prayer group turned me down. Not one. When God, handpicks the people, the people are ones that He knows will respond to Him and pray!

For the joy of the Lord is your strength.

Nehemiah 8:10 (NIV)

Restore to me the joy of your salvation and grant me a willing spirit, to sustain me.

Psalms 51:12 (NIV)

Being confident of this, that he who began a good work in you will carry it on to completion until the day of Christ Jesus.

Philippians 1:6 (NIV)

Your lives are echoing the Master's Word, not only in the provinces but all over the place. The news of your faith in God is out. We don't even have to say anything anymore-you're the message!"

1 Thessalonians 1:8-10 (The Message)

Create in me a pure heart, O God, and renew a steadfast spirit within me.

Psalms 51:10 (NIV)

I tell you the truth, if anyone says to this mountain, "Go, throw yourself into the sea," and does not doubt in his heart but believes that what he says will happen, it will be done for him.

Mark 11:23 (NIV)

Since, then, you have been raised with Christ, set your hearts on things above, where Christ is seated at the right hand of God. Set your minds on things above, not on earthly things.

Colossians 3:1-2 (NIV)

Therefore, since we are surrounded by such a great cloud of witnesses, let us throw off everything that hinders and the sin

that so easily entangles, and let us run with perseverance the race marked out for us.

Hebrews 12:1 (NIV)

That all may honor the Son just as they honor the Father. He who does not honor the Son does not honor the Father, who sent him.

John 5:23 (NIV)

To love him with all your heart, with all your understanding, and with all your strength, and to love your neighbor as yourself is more important than all burnt offerings and sacrifices.

Mark 12:33 (NIV)

Why Am I Going

Someone has asked why I am going to "Target." Why would I risk going to a place that has no tolerance for people who leave Islam and choose Messiah Yeshua (Jesus)? Believe me; I have asked Him that too. But He graciously showed me a lot about the "Target" country. It is a 50/50 chance of being stoned if you get divorced. Stoning is a traditional form of punishment. Your male relatives could choose to commit an honor killing. This is sometimes by stoning, sometimes by drowning, etc., but always resulting in death. It is literally up to how radical or fanatical your male relatives are as to what your punishment will be. If you convert and leave Islam, it is most likely 100% to be stoned or to be put to death. So why go?

In John Chapter 8, the adulterous woman was brought to Him and instead of choosing sides or responding the way the crowd expected, He chose to speak love, forgiveness, and truth. He chose not to pick up a stone. He has shown me that to be truly His; I have to look and do like Him. I have to choose to drop my stone or better yet, to never choose to pick it up. The stone is judgment. It is so easy to pick up a stone, judge another as wrong in our opinion, and hurl it into the air to pronounce judgment and punishment. The stone/judgment will cause damage if it hits the intended target. Even if it misses its mark, it will cause damage in unexpected ways.

God has shown me through prayer that going into a country like "Target," that is dark and in need of His Light, speaking words of love, forgiveness, and His Truth is how He will be glorified. Choosing not to pick up a stone and loving on someone who would pick up a stone to throw at me is what He would do. With all that, He has so graciously given in my life and my children's I have to choose not to pick up that stone because I'm so grateful that He has never chosen to judge me the way I deserve.

"God is love," 1 John 4:16. With all that is going on in our church today, stones are flying everywhere. Some hit the intended targets and some miss and cause unexpected damage. My mother grew up in a Christian home, Many years ago, she left the church because of infighting. She was young, not saved, and saw how the church body beat up on her family members that served the church. It was one of the many reasons she turned away from the church. She decided she wanted nothing to do with people that acted one way and said that they were Christians. She spent 30-35 years in the Islamic faith and raised both of her children in it. Those stones back then did not hit their intended targets of my family members. They hit the children and grandchildren, most of whom walked away from the church. Some have returned, but some have not.

Stones hit, and in my family alone they have influenced major life decisions. I sometimes wonder how different my life would be if Islam were not a part of it. Although I'm grateful for what I've gone through because without it, I would not be saved; I would still be a Muslim. I pray that my brother and his family come to know the Lord personally. Those stones are still affecting him.

We are in the month of Elul on the Jewish calendar. It is a time to repent. I repent right now for my attitude toward the "Target" country. I repent of my hardness toward people that choose to persecute those who love the Lord and choose Him instead of the faith of their parents. I am sorry that I felt anger in that I was raised learning Islamic verses. Instead, I need to be grateful for it because without having been in such darkness, I would not have searched for a source of Light.

I'm so thankful to the God of the Universe for hearing me that night. Thankful to Him who hears when no one else does. In the story of Hagar she calls on the name of God, "The Only One that Hears Me." That name of God is used only once in the Scripture, but it only takes that one time to be heard! God is so good.

Elul is centered on the idea of repentance. Repentance is turning from your old ways to God's ways. The coming holidays of Rosh Hashanah, the Days of Awe, and Yom Kippur mean that we need to prepare ourselves. Elul is a time of introspection, confession, repentance, and restitution.

If someone says, "I love God," and hates his brother, he is a liar; for the one who does not love his brother whom he has seen, cannot love God whom he has not seen. 1 John 4:20 (NASB)

Jesus, Our Messiah, came preaching repentance and reconciliation to God. This time of reflection is to help us stay in balance with the God that is our Creator. He alone can show us through the Holy Spirit where we are self-righteous and full of our fleshy selves.

Looking back, this was as much a declaration to myself as to others who would read it in a prayer update. I was blessed. God told me, "don't hang on to the stone it will make you drown." I let go. I replaced that stone with a letter "d." The letter d was added to my sentence. I let GoD! It's just one letter difference. It's just a stone. Let it go, Shahe!

The scribes and the Pharisees brought a woman caught in adultery, and having set her in the center of the court, they said to Him, "Teacher, this woman has been caught in adultery, in the very act. Now the Law Moses commanded us to stone such women; what then do You say?"

They were saying this, testing Him, so that they might have grounds for accusing Him. But Jesus stooped down and with His finger wrote on the ground. But when they persisted in asking Him, He straightened up and said to them, "He who is without sin among you, let him be the first to throw a stone at her."

Again, He stooped down and wrote on the ground. When they heard it, they began to go out one by one, beginning with the older ones, and He was left alone, and the woman, where she was, in the center of the court.

Straightening up, Jesus said to her, "Woman, where are they? Did not one condemn you?" She said, "No one, Lord." And Jesus said, "I do not condemn you, either. Go. From now on sin no more." John 8 3-11 (NASB)

Second Prayer Update

Prayer for today:

- Pray for our team leader as he makes the final travel arrangements and our visas to be accepted.
- Pray in advance for the Bibles to get in and where they are supposed to go and for the people who will receive them.
- Pray for the persecuted "Target" believers to have endurance and to be able to show the love of Christ to those who oppress them.
- Pray for the people of "Target" that we will encounter in advance that the Lord prepare their hearts.

Father, I pray that I do not hinder the Holy Spirit but keep myself from falling for the lusts of this world. Help me to put your Word into my heart and take the Word into "Target." In Jesus' Name, I pray, Amen.

Rejoice always; pray without ceasing; in everything give thanks; for this is God's will for you in Christ Jesus. Do not quench the Spirit; do not despise prophetic utterances. But examine everything carefully; hold fast to that which is good; abstain from every form of evil. Now may the God of peace Himself sanctify you entirely; and may your spirit and soul and body be preserved complete, without blame at the coming of our Lord Jesus Christ. Faithful is He who calls you, and He also will bring it to pass.

1 Thessalonians 5:16-24 (NASB)

The LORD passed by in front of him and proclaimed, "The LORD, the LORD God, compassionate and gracious, slow to anger; and abounding in lovingkindness and truth; who keeps lovingkindness for thousands, who forgives iniquity, transgression and sin; yet He will by no means leave the guilty unpunished, visiting the iniquity of fathers on the children and on the grandchildren to the third and fourth generations."

Exodus 36:6-7 (NASB)

No Medal

The kids and I take a week off to go to Florida. We drive down. Gas is at its lowest in a long while. So low that we take a picture of the sign. We get to our "cheap" hotel, and they hand us a bunch of coupons which feed us nicely.

The next day we make our way back to Walt Disney World. For one week I want this trip to be all about time with my children. The kids are older now and they are taller. They are tall enough to ride rides that we did not ride before. It is no longer about the characters but the rides. Adam is being brave and trying new things. Last time I had to bribe him with a trip to the gift shop if he would go with me and Aalia into the Spaceship Earth ride at Epcot. I had never been in there before, and I did not know what to expect from the ride. But Adam no longer trusted me with rides.

I made a fatal parenting mistake back in 2002 when we went to Disney. I did not read the guide book early on in the trip. You know, the map that they give you at the entrance. It marks the scary rides and where to get food. I had the map in my hands, but I never opened it up fully to read the bottom. I am a smart person, a know-it-all. I only referred to the map when I needed to know where I was. Aalia, Adam, and I went to the Dinosaur ride because the kids like dinosaurs. I had no idea.

We waited, and we got on board a jeep-like vehicle. Aalia is on one side of me, and Adam is on the other side of me. I have a small backpack full of our snacks, rain ponchos, wallet, and supplies. My net is broken. It does not provide a place to securely put my backpack. Without thinking, I just tuck it between my legs. It's a dark colored bag. It's dark in there, so I don't think the operator saw it. We are rather brown, people!

The ride starts. The kids are smiling, and we think we are going to see dinosaurs. Well, that changes fast. We round the corner and a huge dinosaur yells in our faces. There are lights flashing, screaming noises, and giant dinosaurs trying to kill us. My kids are eight and ten, but they, and I have never seen the JP dinosaur movies. We were in for a ride!

I have forgotten to tell you that our jeep is bumping and thumping and going this way and that to get away from those loud monsters. My backpack is moving so I squeeze my legs tight. Not good enough. I wrap my foot around a strap and secure the bag between my thighs. Oh, and I have forgotten to tell you that both of my children have buried their faces and are screaming into my armpits. I am so ticklish!

We bump and thump and move from terror to terror. Aalia gets brave and sticks her head up to see the next screaming dinosaur and then goes back down. Adam just stays buried and screams. He has been in my arm pit so long that hot air from his screaming has made me sweat. I am laughing from being tickled on both sides by the faces of my babies who are screaming and crying and mad that they see me laughing. They think that I am laughing at them. My arms are around their bodies, and I'm holding on to them for dear life. I don't have time to be scared. My legs ache from squeezing my thighs so tight to hang on to the backpack. It keeps trying to escape with the help of the Jeep. My poor children. My poor armpits. *Please, Lord, help us make it to the end. I don't know if you answer prayers from an amusement ride, but I sure hope you do!*

I am laughing out of control. Three-quarters of that laughter is because I have brown babies screaming into my ticklish armpits and one-quarter is the absurdity of it all. Honestly, people! When you get yourself into this kind of situation all you can do is call upon the Lord and laugh! I get off the ride with wet armpits from sweating and possibly a few of their tears. I walk bow-legged. Next time I will read the guide book! They try to help you. They try to warn you! Who knew? I am convinced that that famous commercial of the mom with her two kids buried in her chest got the idea from the picture that the ride took of us. It was classic, people! I walked funny the rest of the day. My leg muscles ached!

Well, that is why Adam would not go up the Epcot sphere. He no longer trusted me. But that was 2002. It is 2007. We've changed, right? Adam has studied the guide book for Disney. He has made a list of all the places that we "have to go to mom." Aalia and I want to go to the Rockin' Roller Coaster. Adam is fine at first but not so sure. The closer to the ride we get in line, the more nervous he gets. I ask him if he wants to change his mind. He says no.

We are now the next ones to get on board. Adam is having Dinosaur flashbacks. He starts to panic as the group in front of us leaves the docking station. In the dark, I can see the white of his eyes. He is in panic mode. I try to assure him that he will be fine. "You said that last time!" he quickly reminds me. "Don't forget the dinosaurs!" I have wounded my child. I beg and plead and try to convince him to stay. We won't be able to wait in this long line again I reason. It's time. Here comes the car. It seats people two by two.

I ask Aalia if she is fine to be the just one and I will ride next to Adam. She says she's fine. That's my girl! Adam puts one foot in and then panics. I tell him to hurry and get in. We argue, and I snap. Get in! Stop crying; you will be fine! He obeys. I look like the worst parent ever! I'm sure everyone behind me talked about the evil "foreigner that MADE her poor son get on the ride." I promise that I will be right beside him. "You are going to be ok, Adam!" He is freaking out and fusses at me from the docking station until the launch pad…yes, I said launch pad. Who knew?

We launched into the pitch black darkness to the tunes of screaming rock n roll music. You should have seen the picture. Aalia is smiling with excitement. I turn and look at Adam. He has an expression of sheer terror! I promise you that I am not trying to kill my children! I never went to Disney as a child. I am a parent that kind of learns as she goes. It's a whole new world! Is that a Disney song?

He realizes that he has not died and he calms down and starts to get excited. By the end of the ride, he loves it. We get off the ride with all three of us smiling. Adam is sweaty but the first words out of his mouth are, "Can we do it again?" Where are those people, people? You know the ones that bashed me for being a bad parent and snapping at my kid to "get on board." But I knew that if he would just try it, he would survive and, in fact, he would enjoy it. He would want to do it again. Unfortunately, the same people that heard me say that to Adam were currently on the ride and did

77

not see us return. They did not see him beg to do it again. We did do the ride again by the way! That's my boy!

We spend the rest of the trip doing a lot of the most wonderful things together as a family. It is truly a blessing! I enjoy that I can just "be" here with them. Last time my job situation was looming over my head. No more interviewing for a new job in the line of It's A Small World, people! We are blessed at every turn. Our fifty percent off vacation is a hundred percent of a blessing. We have a great time. It is a long ride home to face lots of homework because they missed a week of school. They had a wonderful vacation, and they were ok that they would not get a medal for perfect attendance. It was a perfect week! Tears and all!

When we get home, I catch up on the mission trip details. Our "Kmart" country of entry has been compromised. The secret church groups have been arrested. The in-country contact has been outed. There are people in custody and the enemy seems to have gained the upper hand. We need to make changes to how we do this. We can't go this spring. It's too soon.

Our source for Persian Bibles has also had trouble and is unable to print them and get them to us in-country. It means that we will have to get them once we are in "Target." It is not going to be easy. Now we have to pray about what God wants us to do. We will have to "carry" the burden. I hope you understand that I cannot safely write too many details. I want the chain of access to stay open!

My heart breaks for the Persian believers. They are in great danger. We are spoiled in the American church. I have multiple Bibles and the internet. They have to share a Bible and hide them. They cannot openly live out their faith for fear of being arrested. I wonder if I should continue with the trip. It is getting dangerous.

I have one foot in the door so to speak; there is still time. I can back out. I hear the Lord speak to my heart. He tries to convince me to stay, "We, you and Me, Shahe, won't be able to wait in this long line again." He reasons with me. It is time. Here comes the mission's trip. "I promise to be right beside you. You are going to be ok, Shahe!" I guess I need to be prepared to launch! I need to be brave even if I don't get a medal!

Looking back, God is my Father. And yes, sometimes He says, "That's my girl!" And yes, sometimes He says, "Get in! Stop crying; you will be fine!" And yes, sometimes I just need to trust my parent. Obey my parent! He knows that I will survive and in fact, really enjoy it. I bet He knows that I will want to do it again. He, Father God, is not the worst parent ever! One church painted and one more to go. God is good!

Oh, and in case you missed it. Our mission trip moved from the spring to the fall due to all of the arrests and persecution. Now we will not enter in by "Kmart" and we will go in through another country that we have nick-named "Walmart." Now the trip order happens just like God said it would, "Florida, Target, and Israel!" This Guy is really good!

And your sons will be taught of the LORD; and the well-being of your sons will be great.

Isaiah 54:13 (NASB)

Parenting, Prayer, and Painting

Time is passing, and I am parenting. I am also praying. I am also preparing. I am productive at work. And I am painting. Ugh! I did it again. Foo-foo phrases! I sound like a preacher with all the "p" words! Lord, help me!

Our mission's team is unified. We are having trouble with our visas. I, of course, have trouble with my passport. How am I going to get in with my current passport that says that I have been to Israel two times in the past two years? The government of "Target" wants to wipe the people of Israel off of the map! Now add in that I also plan to return to Israel in the fall. Do you expect an open welcome in Israel if I have been to the country of "Target?" You know, the one that wants to wipe Israel off of the face of the map. Well, if you thought I had past security issues in Israel, just you wait and see! I picture detector wands of all shapes, sizes, and colors. I picture x-rays of my x-rays. I picture plastic gloves and body cavity searches! It's getting ugly, people! I apply for a second passport. This time, I have to wear a head scarf and cover my evil hair to get my visa approved! UGH! I hate head scarves!

The previous day, I pulled up to the school to pick up my children, and it was Adam's fourteenth birthday. He had the first football game of the season later that evening, and he was starting defensive lineman. You could see by his smile that "it is a wonderful world." I got to the hilltop of the school yard and saw smoke. I thought it must be construction burning. I then rounded the corner, and it was the tree line burning between my Children's private school and the public middle school next door. A transformer blew, sparks flew, and flames ignited the dry brush and trees that in the past had divided the two properties.

In an instant because it was dismissal time and the power was out the children were evacuated; cars were in the parking lot next to the burning trees and children were everywhere. That's when I saw individuals become united team players. Parents herded children into safety; other parents started asking for help to identify cars parked next to the flames (this was the area students park in). Other parents (like me) called their kids and told them to get car keys for the friends' cars. The teachers got the keys and moved the vehicles.

The flames were above the tree tops and moving in the strong wind very quickly. Within an instant, the "body" of Christ was unified. Safety of children was first, cars and school buses second. I helped drive and move a school bus, and, yes, I could reach the gas pedal. Others moved other things. It was amazing.

But the cool part was the kids. Some started praying. There was a fuel tank in the forwarding path of the flames, and kids were helping other kids get in contact with their parents who were stuck in traffic. All of the areas around the two schools lost electricity and traffic backed up on the main road. Parents were panicked because the radio said that the school was burning not the tree line. The kids then started praying for the other kids in the school next door.

When it was all done, you saw firefighters and emergency management folks knocking themselves out and doing an amazing job to prevent the quick-spreading fire from getting to the two schools. In the middle of flames, a man on an open cab bulldozer began making a trench between the flames to cut off the fire spread while the fire trucks surrounded the fire by putting themselves between the flames and the schools. Everyone was helping, even bringing cold water to the firefighters.

It made me think that in "times of stress/crises" when the heat and flames are turned up, where are you in your walk? Do you pick up your kids, put them in the car, figure that you are safe and leave the situation and go on to the store and find out in the morning the gossipy details? Do you participate? Do you stand by and let others do the work? Do you get in the way of the work that needs to be done? Do you offer refreshment in times of great stress? Do you put yourself in danger to keep younger ones out of it? Do you leave the scene and exaggerate on what you did or didn't do in conversations with others? Do you step into the gap between the flames and life? Do you call on the name of the Lord? These are hard questions to ask yourself.

The previous night, I went to a ball game and watched my now fourteen-year-old son play in the heat with a giant smile on his face. He would hit someone and hold out a hand to pick them up after he hit them. At the end of the game, after they do the line down the middle to shake hands, they circle up to pray. At first, it was two separate circles. Then someone in the middle, probably our coach (godly individual that makes daily impacts on young people), gathered them all up into one united big circle, on their knees to pray with the team players mixing in with one another.

In times like these with the heat turned up in more ways than the temperature, we need to stick together. When one of us is knocked down for a moment, extend that hand to help them up, be joyful in everything, smile as if it was your 14th birthday and you got to be a starting lineman on the football team. Be a cheerleader and encourage God's team. Offer refreshment in the Living Water. Be united, willing to get on our knees and pray in unity to the Lord God Almighty, the Author of the Universe. That's the kind of picture that you can't help but wonder if God does look at and say, "It's a wonderful world I've created."

Looking back, I can't help but think that it is a wonderful world that God has made. Now all of these years later since the trip, there are some answered prayers that have come to light that were prayed for including that new believers have satellite and internet access to programs that feed them in their language. Praise the Lord! Closed areas that were once closed and dark have become open and with the Light of the World. Praise the Lord! Persian Bibles have made it into the country. Praise the Lord! People are getting saved every day. Praise the Lord!

Let everything that has breath, praise the LORD. Praise the LORD!

Psalm 150:6 (NASB)

Third Prayer Update:

Prayer for Target:

- Pray for the reopening of the source for Persian Bibles in "Target." What a blessing it would be to have the Scriptures readily available again in "Target!"
- Pray that the new believers will learn to listen to God by reading the Word and applying it.
- Some believers do not have a fellowship to attend. Pray that they will get encouragement from radio broadcasts, Scripture portions, or other Christian literature.
- Pray for a massive people movement among the 5,000,000 "Target" tribal people of southwest "Target" with many coming to trust in Christ.
- Pray for the safety of those that were arrested and persecuted.

Prayer for the team:

- Pray for team leader and making plans to travel.
- Pray for visas to be accepted.
- Pray for a possible short trip to get training that we make the right decision for our team.
- Pray for our mission contacts in the "Kmart, Walmart, and Target" countries.
- Pray for receptive and prepared hearts in the "Target" country.
- Pray for team UNITY.

Father, help me to see You in everything and respond with the joy of the Lord. Help me to be usable by You. In Jesus' Name, I pray, Amen.

How good and pleasant it is when brothers live together in unity! It is like precious oil poured on the head, running down on the beard, running down on Aaron's beard, down upon the collar of his robes. It is as if the dew of Hermon were falling on

Mount Zion. For there the Lord bestows his blessing, even life forevermore.

Psalm 133 (NIV)

Finally, all of you, live in harmony with one another; be sympathetic, love as brothers, be compassionate and humble. Do not repay evil with evil or insult with insult, but with blessing, because to this you were called so that you may inherit a blessing. For, "Whoever would love life and see good days must keep his tongue from evil and his lips from deceitful speech. He must turn from evil and do good; he must seek peace and pursue it. For the eyes of the Lord are on the righteous and his ears are attentive to their prayer, but the face of the Lord is against those who do evil." Who is going to harm you if you are eager to do good? But even if you should suffer for what is right, you are blessed. Do not fear what they fear; do not be frightened. But in your hearts set apart Christ as Lord. Always be prepared to give an answer to everyone who asks you to give the reason for the hope that you have. But do this with gentleness and respect.

1 Peter 3:8-15 (NIV)

For the joy of the Lord is your strength.

Nehemiah 8:10

We Are In A Drought

Last night, I got home from my ladies Bible Study and got the kids ready for bed and went outside to water my flowers. The flowers are looking sad. Normally, when all is well, I have flower beds full of all kinds of flowers in lots of different colors. I started to look around me as I watered. The grass is brown and dead, in one area on my bank, it is already just dirt, so dry that the crabgrass is dead. In the silence of the night, the leaves on the trees can be heard falling off the trees because they are brown, and they make a crunching noise as they hit the ground. When I watered my flower bed in the front, instead of the water sinking into the ground, the ground was so dry that the water lifted up the dirt and it washed the dirt off onto the sidewalk. There went the soil and I watched it float down the driveway. It washed away so quickly. There went the nutrients; the stuff that lets life grow in it. It is gone. Instead of it being in a flower bed and being useful as a mass of dirt it was now spread out over the driveway. Tomorrow morning the water will have dried up, and the wind will blow the small pieces away like dust. The dust has a history, but no one ever stops to wonder what that dust was once a part of because now it is dust, useless and in the way, swept or polished off of something. Discarded.

The flowers were hurting too. During the hottest part of the one-hundred-degree weather, I had asked the kids to help me water the plants. I had a hard time breathing in the hot weather and was careful during bad air quality days because of my asthma. Both just rushed through the process of watering. To the kids it was a chore; to me, it is my time with God. The plants showed the difference. When the kids were watering them, they were slightly nourished, but suffering because they were not watered deeply at the roots. When I began watering them, there was a major difference, and the blooms started coming back.

All of this last night made me think of relationships around me. How often do I treat relationships and water them like Aalia or Adam and make the relationship a chore versus taking time and loving and watering the relationship deeply at the roots? It is so easy to run around and "play" social and not make any real impact on the relationships around us. How often does God want us to slow down, not make it a chore but a joy to share His Living Water with those around us? It is so easy when you slack off and don't spend consistent time with God in prayer and reading of His Word that you can go from green and blossoming to dry and dusty. How often do we let circumstances get in the way and allow it to take away our nutrients and ability to grow something within? Sometimes we are guilty of letting life wash us down a driveway.

I encourage you today to make time with God first, read His Word, pray and talk to Him. Drink Him in deeply all the way to the roots. Allow Him to nourish you and you, in turn, nourish those around you that are still drinking from shallow waters. Make it a priority to hide His Word in your heart so that when the drought comes you can survive because you have made strong roots that drink deeply. Don't let others sweep you away with the flow if the flow is not in God's direction. If you find yourself drying out on the driveway, call your friend and ask for prayer and conversation, encouragement to lift your spirit so that you don't dry up like dust. Did you know that the vast majority of dust in a home comes off of the human body? No one God ever created was meant to be discarded.

I got up this morning with the idea to give up and slim down activities in my life so that I can be more purposeful in my relationships instead of so spread out. He does stuff for a reason and extremes make you appreciate the ordinary. God likes to use ordinary!

Looking back, I know that prayers are being prayed because there is such a sense of peace in this process. Drought is a time to reevaluate. You must purpose yourself to drink the Living Water. He alone will refresh you. My home church was starting to shows signs of cracking and splitting. Our land was dry. The ground was dry. Our hearts were dry too.

Jesus answered and said to her, "Everyone who drinks of this water will thirst again; but whoever drinks of the water that I will give him will become in him a well of water springing up to eternal life."

John 4:13-14 (NASB)

He who believes in Me, as the Scripture said, "From his innermost being will flow rivers of living water."

John 7:38 (NASB)

Therefore you will joyously draw water from the springs of salvation.

Isaiah 12:3 (NASB)

Fourth Prayer Update

Prayer for Target:

- Pray that some living outside of "Target" who have come to Christ might desire to return to reach their relatives, as well as reach out to others. This could include visits, or returning permanently to "Target." Pray that they might be bold in proclaiming their faith in Jesus Christ.
- Pray that President of "Target" and others in the Islamic "Target" government will lead the country with wisdom. The Bible tells us to pray for those in authority so that Christian Believers may lead peaceful and quiet lives in all godliness and holiness.
- Pray that believers will stand firm in their walk with God at home, work, and school and be able to testify wisely about their faith in Jesus Christ.
- Ask God to help you pray for needs that only the Holy Spirit can reveal to you.

Praise to celebrate!

- Praise God! We have plane tickets in hand and finally set dates for the trip.
- We leave October 10th, 2007. Ten is a very good number. Complete!
- My brother and his wife got to hear their baby's heartbeat yesterday! God is good!

Prayer for the team:

- Pray now for the "Target" country's tourist agency to provide our team leader with the number needed to attach to our visas.
- Pray for the visa process and that they are accepted.
- Pray for our team as we go to a "City, State" in September for training to take Bibles into our "Target" country.
- Pray now for those Bibles to get to those who will need them in the "Target" country.

- Pray for our missionary contact that will meet us in "State" and then in our staging country ("Walmart") and go in with us into "Target." Pray for their family also.
- Pray for team unity.
- Pray for the team to be willing to go through the "process" of preparation that God will do as He prepares us for His work.

Father, heal the dry places that crack and allow the enemy of my soul to come in. Fill my thirst with You. Help me to be usable by You! In Jesus' Name, I pray, Amen.

O God, You are my God; I shall seek You earnestly; my soul thirsts for You, my flesh yearns for You, in a dry and weary land where there is no water. Thus I have seen You in the sanctuary, to see Your power and Your glory. Because Your lovingkindness is better than life, my lips will praise You. So I will bless You as long as I live; I will lift up my hands in Your name. My soul is satisfied as with marrow and fatness, and my mouth offers praises with joyful lips. When I remember You on my bed, I meditate on You in the night watches, for You have been my help, and in the shadow of Your wings I sing for joy. My soul clings to You; Your right hand upholds me.

Psalm 63:1-8 (NASB)

I Will Praise You In The Storm

Today is the two-year anniversary of Hurricane Katrina. Two years ago the New Orleans area and surrounding communities were devastated. There was controversy, division, pain, bad attitudes, hurt feelings, wrongs, apathy, tears, fears, loss, lack of communication, and abundance of communication. In the midst of this was a song that Casting Crowns put out called, "I Will Praise Him In The Storm." They didn't know that Katrina would hit when the song was released, but God did!

What do Katrina and this song have to do with each other? Well, I don't remember ever praying for New Orleans or the surrounding area before Katrina. The storm caused me to wake up to what was going on in that part of the country; it caused me to pray, to do "something" and to seek God in the situation. It caused me to realize that I was, in a sense, a part of the "times in which this event was happening" It also helped me to realize that I could do no more than pray, seek God, and volunteer in some manner of relief. I was simply not in control.

It is in many ways the same with my home church, although I realize that I am a part of the times in which all this is happening, I also realize that I can do no more than to pray, seek God, and volunteer in some manner of relief. I am not in control. God is.

I am going to do another of my "I will never do that." I have bullet points. My church is hurting. It seems appropriate to use because bullets cause pain. I am in pain.

I will praise you in the storm:

- Without this storm, we would not change because times are changing.
- Without this storm, we would not reposition ourselves to fit into God's plan because we would be content to be where we were, comfortable and in our world.
- Without this storm, we would not be seeking God in the midst of the storm.

90

- Without this storm, we would not be offering up prayers for unity.
- Without this storm, we would not be praying for our church, our pastor, our staff, our members the way we are now.
- Without this storm, we would not be as passionate as we are now.
- Without this storm, we would not be stepping up to the plate in new ways to fill in for losses.
- Without this storm, we would not appreciate our relationships at church as much.
- Without this storm, we would not be so purposeful in our conversations, thoughts, actions, etc.
- Without this storm, we would not be as grateful for our church.
- Without this storm, we would not be as broken.
- Without this storm, we would not be in a position of repentance.
- Without this storm, we would not be hurting.
- Without this storm, we would not shed tears and be cleansed.
- Without this storm, we would not celebrate the little things and the big things.
- Without this storm, we would not hang on to the hem of His garment for healing.
- Without this storm, we would be doing our own thing and thinking that we can do it on our own without God.
- Without this storm, we would be in a selfish place instead of selfless.

This list can go on and on.

I praise God that sometimes He sends the storm to wake us up, make us aware that prayer and repentance, fasting, tears, joy, etc. are all a part of the process of staying in intimate conversation with the Lord God Almighty. He wants us to be a part of His work and what He is doing.

Without this trip to the "Target" country, I can honestly say that I have never prayed for the Persian speaking world as much as I have since God said to me that I was going on the mission field. I was sleeping right through what He was doing there. He wants me to be a part of His doings there; He wants to be in intimate conversation with me about what He is doing because that's what friends do. We tell each other everything.

Fill in the blank related to your life.

Right now in my life, the storm which is _____, is causing me great stress, great controversy, tears, anger, division, hurt feelings, etc. But I'm going to choose to praise Him in the storm because He is who He is and no matter where I am, and every tear I cry, He holds me in His hand. He never left my side, and though my heart is torn, I will praise Him in this storm.

Looking back, my favorite line is "I lift my eyes unto the hills, where does my help come from, my help comes from the Lord the Maker of Heaven and Earth." Yup, He is!

Leaving the crowd, they took Him along with them in the boat, just as He was; and other boats were with Him. And there arose a fierce gale of wind, and the waves were breaking over the boat so much that the boat was already filling up.

Jesus Himself was in the stern, asleep on the cushion; and they woke Him and said to Him, "Teacher, do You not care that we are perishing?"

And He got up and rebuked the wind and said to the sea, "Hush, be still." And the wind died down and it became perfectly calm. And he said to them, "Why are you afraid?" Do you still have no faith?"

They became very much afraid and said to one another, "Who then is this, that even the wind and the sea obey Him?"

Mark 4:36-41 (NASB)

Fifth Prayer Update

I hadn't planned to email this morning, but this is what God was showing me, and I need to "sing His praises!"

- I sing His praises for what He is doing in our church right now.
- I sing His praises for how He is sifting us, how He is shifting us, and how He is changing us!
- I sing His praises for how people are coming and going.
- I sing His praises for the losses and the gains.
- I sing His praises for the controversy and the pain.
- I sing His praises for the division.
- I sing His praises for the bad attitudes and the hurt feelings.
- I sing His praises for the wrongs that have been committed.
- I sing His praises for the apathy.
- I sing His praises for the "hot under the collar" emotions that rise.
- I sing His praises for the tears and the fears.
- I sing His praises for the stubbornness and the pride-fullness.
- I sing His praises for the lack of communication and abundance of communication.

This list can go on and on.

Father, my prayer for today is that I would respond in praise to You with any storm that comes my way. I pray that I will sing Your praises when no one else wants too! Help me to be usable by You! I pray this in Jesus' Name, Amen.

Great is the LORD, and highly to be praised, and His greatness is unsearchable.

Psalm 145:3 (NASB)

Trust Me

Wednesday night the kids and I arrived home at about 9:30 pm. On my doorstep was a FedEx package. I had no idea what it was. I got inside and opened it up to find my plane ticket and travel information to Israel. I was astonished and somewhat angry.

I couldn't help but think that the package had been there all day, in plain view of traffic and passersby, and it could be stolen. Especially on Wednesdays which are such long days for our family. We have had toy water guns stolen off of that front porch. I thanked God for guarding it and for no one taking it. I went to bed still thinking how amazing it was that it was not stolen.

The next morning, we were going out the door to school and out of nowhere a man that we had never seen before walked right up to us and the car, passed us up without speaking, walked across the front walkway of our house and kept walking toward the main road. My mind went angrily right away to "See God, anyone and everyone passes my porch, how could my ticket just be laying there all day!"

His reply was quick, "I can blind the eyes of those I choose to. If I choose for something not to be seen then it will not be seen. Trust me." Ok. I am mush.

For the Bibles that we are taking in, I asked Him for prayers to trust the Lord, to trust Him that He is in control and that He blinds the eyes of those He chooses to blind.

This morning is different because my mother calls me to tell me she was reading, and she has a Bible verse for me today. She immediately thought of me when she read it. It brought her a sense of purpose and comfort. She knows that this trip is meant to be for me.

Then I will set the key of the house of David on his shoulder, when he opens no one will shut, when he shuts no one will open.

Isaiah 22:22 (NASB)

I know it may seem strange to you because maybe you are used to your mom quoting you Scripture. I am not. In fact, I think this is the first time she has ever said she had a verse for me. ME!

The enemy may have "blinded our eyes or closed doors in the past with Islam, but God, the Maker of Heaven and Earth, can change all that! My mother is a believer now. How cool is God!

Looking back, how can you not trust a God that says that He can open the eyes of the ones He chooses to open and close the eyes of the ones He chooses to close. He follows it up with a loving but firm Fatherly God kind of way, "Trust Me."

I pray that the eyes of your heart may be enlightened, so that you will know what is the hope of His calling, what are the riches of the glory of His inheritance in the saints.

Ephesians 1:18 (NASB)

Sixth Prayer Update

Prayer for Target:

- Pray for the people who live along the Caspian Sea live almost 3,000,000 Muslim people who have yet to hear the Gospel.
- Pray for someone to reach out to these people.
- Pray that the Persian radio signals into "Target" will meet no interference and that the programs will come in clearly.
- Pray, that programs are in the mother tongue.
- Pray, that fellowship groups will be started.
- Pray for the former Muslim background believers cannot attend the churches remaining in "Target." Believers are scared. It difficult for new believers to grow. Pray for the Spirit of God to help them in their new-found faith.
- Pray for the numerous churches and fellowships of "Target" people meet outside of "Target" throughout Europe, the U.S., Canada, Australia, and parts of Asia.
- Pray for the pastors and leaders as they reach out to dispersed people from "Target."
- Pray for the 65% of the population of "Target" which is under 25 years of age. Minds need to be captured with the cause of Christ. New, creative ideas are needed.

Prayer for the team:

- Pray for our visa's to be approved.
- Pray for guidance and unity as the team meets this Sunday.
- Pray for preparation and safety traveling on Sunday to City, State to get training on how to take the literature into the "Target" country.
- Pray for the Children's Worship Team that will have to fill in during my absence.
- Pray for the hearts of those we will come into contact with in the "Target" country.
- Pray for the Holy Spirit to go ahead of us and speak in dreams to the Muslims in the "Target" country. Dreams are

important over there, and the Spirit can minister to their hearts in mighty ways!

- Pray for me to get my head on straight with the two trips. I am filled with such joy that it is hard to focus. I anticipate God to move mountains and in mighty ways, and it is hard to focus on the details of today, and there are lots of them.
- Pray, for me to have peace. Amani (ah-Mah-nee) means peace.

Father God, help us to say and live out, "Thy Will be done on earth as it is in heaven." In Jesus' Name, I pray, Amen.

And the peace of God, which transcends all understanding, will guard your hearts and minds through Christ Jesus.

Philippians 4:7 (NIV)

He has showed you, O man, what is good. And what does the Lord require of you? To act justly and to love mercy and to walk humbly with your God.

Micah 6:8 (NIV)

Provision

Last night, I was meditating on "provision." Specifically, God's provision to us. I have marveled how He has pulled the small pieces together and as I get to see slowly a picture forming. It makes me think of provision. He provides. He is God. He is so intimate that sometimes in our fleshiness, we forget how much He provides.

I painted a picture last night of trees and hills in Israel. My mind wandered into God as my paint brush moved. I watched blues blend. Then greens. I put bright yellows on buildings. I then did the unexpected and put some pink on some buildings. As I let my eyes, my hands and the brush wander on the painting, I began to see "a flow."

Without much thought as to measuring, planning, etc. I just started writing the verse from Isaiah 55:12-13. It is a long verse, and it is permanent paint. I can't make a mistake. But it fits. No measurements, no ability of my own, no skill or talent, no not anything of me, I refuse to take credit. The letters just fell onto the picture so effortlessly that I stepped back in awe of how not one more letter could be painted. It just flowed.

It was peace. Something about this picture speaks peace. It flows. God flows. God doesn't make mistakes. He is a redeemer of mistakes we make.

It will be hard to hand it over, in fact, I look over at it sitting on my office chair and feel a small loss. That picture and I flowed. We found peace together.

His provision is peace. It's up to us to let it flow!

Looking back, I am so thankful for people who are praying. Especially, praying for peace. The original 50 prayer warriors have grown. I've stopped counting, but I have been blessed by the prayers in more ways than I could ever express with words.

For you will go out with joy and be led forth with peace; the mountains and the hills will break forth into shouts of joy before you, and all the trees of the field will clap their hands.

Instead of the thorn bush the cypress will come up, and instead of the nettle the myrtle will come up, and it will be a memorial to the LORD, for an everlasting sign which will not be cut off.

Isaiah 55:12-13 (NASB)

Seventh Prayer Update

Prayer for Target:

- Pray for the doors of "Target" to open so that Christian workers, including Persians, might again be able to go in and give out the message.
- Pray that fear of discovery might not deter the home groups from meeting in some cities.
- Pray for consistency and character development for new believers who are being discipled.
- Pray for the Holy Spirit to minister to the Muslim populations in dreams and prepare their hearts in advance.

Prayer for the team:

- Pray for traveling safety as we go early Sunday morning to City, State and back again to learn how to distribute the literature in the "Target" country.
- Pray for team unity.
- Pray that God's will be our focus.
- Pray that we be in a place of flexibility and surrender.
- Pray for the trip that we have traveling safety in and back.
- Pray for the trip that we be usable by God to do whatever He wants.
- Pray for the trip that we be able to bring as many pieces of literature in as possible. (Luke 1:37!)

Father God, thank you for providing for this trip, and I don't just mean financially. Thank you for providing a way when there was no way. Thank you for providing health and safety. Thank you for providing workers and providing the work You wish us to do. Thank you for providing You in every part of this trip. I love You! In Jesus' Name, I pray, Amen!

You will seek me and find me. When you seek me with all your heart.

Jeremiah 29:13 (NIV)

Tuesday

How do you start to write when God is so big!

Let's start by looking at my shoes! If you were to walk in my shoes, you would be praying, juggling, painting, parenting, working, cleaning, preparing. I ask God, "Why are these activities so heavy right now? Why are my shoes so full?" Why can't my shoes go where I want them to go? I want to go on the mission field! I want my shoes to be there now, in fact, I want to be in "Target" and even in Israel. NOW!

Then you hear a strong voice, parent-like, speaking to a beloved child. Take your shoes off. This is Holy Ground. Tuesday morning I call in sick to work. And I take off my shoes and step into His Holiness.

I worship and pray and read His precious word, and He just fills me up. To my mission team, I apologize in advance and ask forgiveness for my words. I questions, "How can I go on a mission trip with people that don't know what they are up against?" We had a discussion in the car yesterday as to who Allah is. I believe that he is the moon god and a false god. He is not and could never be the Everlasting Father who created the universe and is God Almighty the Living God. Allah lays false claims to being the One True God.

How can you go into battle without first identifying your enemy? Our enemy is Lucifer. He has a spirit of darkness that reigns in the Muslim world. If I could, I would purposely not capitalize Allah, Muslim, or Islam. I choose to diminish their importance. There is an evil principality that is the "Prince of Persia." (Daniel 10:13, 20)

In battle, you must know your enemy, and know where to swing your sword. If you don't, you will waste all of your energy swinging in all directions without any direct hit. You live in fear and swing randomly at anything that just seems to move. You may even look like you are swinging your sword in the wind. You are relying on what you see or feel with your ability and rely on your body.

When you fight a known enemy, the prince of darkness, you fight with the sword of the Lord. You swing with His Spirit and Word and Strength. You swing with purpose. You swing in fear of the Lord and not the enemy. You swing where God tells you. You swing how He tells you. You swing at what He tells you. You hit your target. Satan is the target in the country of "Target."

I spend the morning in His Word with Him showing me new places in Isaiah 14 that identify Allah as the moon god. After three hours, I am exhausted, and I feel Him say that I should rest. In the quiet, I suddenly reach over to the remote control and flip on the TV. It is Noon, and the half-hour program started on international prophecy conference, and the man whom I've never heard of begins his teaching time with, "Let me tell you how Satan is deceiving the people; Allah is not Jehovah, he is the moon god." I about fell out of the couch. For thirty minutes, it is as if this man had summarized my three hours with God into a thirty-minute teaching. I just sit and cry and praise God. Then I say to God, "But what do I do with this?" He says to pray for a teaching time with your team to reveal the enemy and prepare for battle.

Another question I pose Tuesday morning is "Lord, why is it that all summer I have wanted to paint at the other church, why is it only now, at such a busy time in preparation for the trips that I am painting?" Again, I'm shoeless. "The Son Church" has blessed me by providing for this trip in exchange for artwork. (I have changed the church's name for security reasons)

Part of the artwork includes twenty-six canvases. One for each letter of the alphabet. Their children will be committing these verses to memory in the next year. The walls around the canvases are mission related. I have painted the names of Jesus in many different languages. I have to paint a canvas a day to complete the job in time. God graciously reveals to me that part of my preparation is to memorize these Scriptures.

When I paint, part of the process is to pray about what I am going to paint. I pray about what colors to use. I pray about what to or not to put on the canvas. When I paint Scripture, I tend to memorize it as it goes onto the canvas. There is a neat side-effect to painting. When I need that Scripture in daily life, I just think of that painting, and I can remember the painted words.

Well, it hit me as I type that today is twenty-six days until the trip, there are twenty-six verses. God is moving! The "Son Church" is "training their children up in the way they should go!"

Another question is, "How much of me do I take on this trip? By me, I also mean, my "needs." What items do I pack that I can't live without? My "wants" are items that I pack that I can't live without. They are my "have-to-haves." You know the ones! Well again, looking at naked feet...He clearly revealed in a process... "How much are you willing to be put out? Are you willing to be put out of your conveniences, your needs, your desires, and your stuff? How much of your "stuff" are you willing to let go of or leave behind? How much room are you going to make for Me?"

Ok, you might not get this yet. Let me tell you about the suitcases. The less we pack of our stuff, the more of Him gets in. Let me go a bit more into detail. This is big, people! The more of my items in my suitcases that I choose to leave behind or not bring at all, the more room there will be in my suitcase for Him. The more I choose to do without or the more I choose to be inconvenienced, the more room there will be in my suitcase for Him. The less stuff I need means that my bags, my luggage, can have more room in them for His Word. "How much room am I going to let Him have?" Well, let's get real here, as I am trying to put my shoes on and tie some shoelaces...I gotta have some stuff, don't I? BAM! He hits me so hard it knocks my shoes off.

In the past, God began speaking to me about "drink offering." Did you even read the second book, people? In short, a drink offering is mature wine poured out at the altar of sacrifice solely for the Lord's pleasure. It is an offering that you choose to do. It is not a "tithe" type that you have to do, but an "offering" type which is one that you go out of your way to acquire. The wine for the offering in the old days would cost several months or years' worth of wages. This wine would be poured out to the Lord. God was showing me that the more I allowed Him to empty "me" out, the more He could fill me up with Him.

Pop back to the picture of me sitting there trying to put shoes on "fleshy feet" in the presence of the Most High God. He said, "I've been preparing you since that time to be a drink offering, empty of yourself, be filled up with Me, mature wine, an offering solely for My pleasure." At that time He first started teaching me, He was teaching me by using a vessel that was a beautiful glass. Now the vessel is both, my luggage and my mind, body, spirit. As I fumble to find my shoes, I realize that my fleshy feet don't need them anymore. There is freedom from the shoes! There is freedom in the Holiness of who Christ Jesus is, was, and will be!

I praise God! God is moving in such big and small ways, and the change is good.

Looking back, I guess I deserved that! I needed to get my shoes knocked off. I better reevaluate "my stuff" and pray about what to pack. I need to make lots and lots of room for Him!

The next morning our team leader emailed out an article on Allah, the moon god and asked in a later email if I would teach the next meeting. He did not know my Tuesday, but God did. God is a mighty God. He gave me back my peace, He is moving and preparing our team for battle, He provides, He is consistent and everlasting! He alone is worthy to be praised.

How you have fallen from heaven, O star of the morning, son of the dawn! You have been cut down to the earth, you who have weakened the nations! But you have said in your heart, I will ascend to heaven; I will raise my throne above the stars of God, and I will sit on the mount of assembly in the recesses of the north.

Isaiah 14:12-13 (NASB)

Eighth Prayer Update

Prayer for Target:

- Pray for the protection of pastors in "Target" as they struggle to lead their flocks in spite of all the restrictions on the Christian faith from the government.
- Pray that A******* and A******* Church members would truly know Jesus Christ as their Lord and Savior and give a good witness to the surrounding Persian population.
- Pray that "freedom of worship" would be the rule in "Target."
- Pray that the Islamic government officials who say that there is freedom for all to worship even though that is not true for the former Muslim background believer.
- Pray that God would raise up a mighty army of prayer warriors for the Persian-speaking world. Perhaps you should be one of them.
- Pray for those who have heard the Word of God today in "Target" and are pondering the claims of Christ. May they say "yes" to Him.
- Pray that pastors and leaders in "Target" would not continue to leave the country. It is very hard to stay, but they are desperately needed.
- Pray that the 50-60 unreached people groups in "Target" will have an opportunity to hear the Gospel in their mother tongue.
- Pray for "Target" believers who are seeking believing spouses. This can be difficult and frustrating. Pray for patience and the willingness to wait on the Lord.

Pray for the team:

- Pray that we get our tourist number and our visas are accepted.
- Pray for team unity.
- Pray for wisdom in into battle. Wisdom to lean on Him, and not ourselves.

- Pray that we be in a posture of prayer and intercession.
- Pray that we be willing to be clean vessels.
- Pray for our families to have security, safety, and good health while we are gone. That they be in place of protection from the enemy.
- Pray for the twenty-six days until the trip

Father God, thank you for giving me Isaiah 55:1-5 as my verses for my traveling in 2007 to Florida, "Target," and Israel. I love Your Word! Verse 55:5 especially gets to me. Thank you for loving me! I pray this in Jesus' name, Amen!

Ho! Every one who thirsts, come to the waters; and you who have no money come, buy and eat. Come, buy wine and milk without money and without cost.

Why do you spend money for what is not bread, and your wages for what does not satisfy? Listen carefully to Me, and eat what is good, and delight yourself in abundance.

Incline your ear and come to Me. Listen that you may live; and I will make an everlasting covenant with you, according to the faithful mercies shown to David.

Behold, I have made him a witness to the peoples, a leader and commander for the peoples.

Behold, you will call a nation you do not know, and a nation which knows you not will run to you, because of the LORD your God, even the Holy One of Israel; for He has glorified you.

Isaiah 55:1-5 (NASB)

Not That City!

My home church is buckling and flailing. My home church is divided. Our division makes the local news. This morning my ex-husband calls and he is concerned about what he has heard on the news about my home church. He asks if I am getting sued. I said no. While he talks, I think how sad that his exposure to church today is this subject of division. Division is a tool of Satan. I start to think that today, specifically today, that I will ask everyone I know to pray for him and his family. Pray for them to be touched by God in a mighty way so that the love of God is greater and has a higher impact on him than a TV segment. So please pray for him and his family today, he needs the salvation that Christ Jesus alone can give.

Of course, he ended the conversation with, if we would just move to *that city* you wouldn't have to work at the church anymore. You could be a teacher in the schools there teaching English.

God is good. He has got a sense of humor! In times like these, let's not forget that we should look like Him!

I want to share with you an omer of manna. When the trip was planned to go to the "Target" country, we were to go to a staging country first. Only in the last few weeks did that country change and specifically list a *certain city*. When I heard the change, I could not help but look up and expect to see God smiling at me. You see, I have said for almost twenty years that I would not go to *that city*. Not just any city, that one!

There are hundreds of cities to choose from and why does it have to be that one? In fact, for six years of marriage, I did not want to go to *that city* every time my husband asked. Then we were divorced. He continued to ask me to go with him to *that city*. I replied that I would not be when we were married and I will not while we are divorced. Even when he remarried, he continued to make comments that we should all go to *that city*.

The last time he commented about *that city* was one week before I found out that our city had changed to *that city!* Again in disbelief, I would answer no. For twenty years total I have said no! It is 2007. He started asking me to go in 1987, people! I told my earthly husband who would become my earthly ex-husband that I would never go there, and I meant it! I told my Heavenly Husband no in a most defiant way too! If you are still for a moment, wait for it…yup! You can still hear the echo of the slap upside the back of my head. Never say never to God! Just send the "I told you so's to my room where I'm staying under the name of Jonah."

The Lord hid this from me until the very latest possible moment because He knows and intimately understands me. I would have bailed, people! All of the prayers, all of the preparation, all of the plans, all out the door if I had one whisper of the name of *that city.* God knew that. He knows me. Now, He has spent months emptying me out. He has unpacked my suitcases. He had unpacked my suitcases again when I tried to put more of my stuff back in there. He has done a "good work" in me and well. UGH! I am going to *that city!*

I find myself thinking, "Come on, God! Have a heart! Give me a break!" Insert stubborn stomping and crossed arms here. I am in toddler mode! He does it again. He reminds me. He reminds me that as I prepare my heart for these trips, He is teaching me to pack up my heart with Him and not me. God is showing me some important elements that are part of my intimate relationship with Him.

Did you know that the heart is the only organ in the human body that does not have to obey the brain? Did you know that the measurements between the cherubim on the mercy seat are similar to the measurements of the human chest cavity? The mercy seat is on top of the ark. The human heart and the ark have something in common. I read once that the ark represents the human heart. The deepest and most intimate part of who we are is our heart. Our heart is the place where the glory of God can take up residence. God alone can transform our hearts. The ark was covered in solid gold on both the inside and the outside. Gold represents the perfected union of God and man.

Inside the Ark of the Covenant are three important elements:

1. The testimonial tablets represent the Word of God manifested in your life. God needs His word to be living out in me and in what "me" does in my daily life. How I live and make decisions in my life, reflect the Word of God in my heart.

2. Aaron's rod which budded is a symbol of rebellion to God-given authority. If I walk in rebellion, then I will walk out a penalty. If I walk in obedience, then I will not only stand against rebellion to the Lord, but I will be willing for His Will to reign in my heart. How I live and make decisions in my life reflects my willingness to submit to the authority of God in my heart.

3. An omer of manna, which represents supernatural provision and freedom from bondage. Manna is bread from heaven to those in the wilderness who had to depend on God and not man for food. The Hebrew people were in the wilderness because God freed them from the Egyptians. I need to trust the Lord with everything in my heart because He alone will supply my needs according to His riches in glory. How I live and make decisions in my life reflects what will be my level of trust in the Lord.

When one of these items was missing during the second Temple era, the ark could not be in the temple. The ark housed the glory of God when all three elements were maintained inside.

I want, no, desire, for my heart to house the glory of God. I want to be in perfect union with Him. He is allowing me to learn how.

For the last couple of weeks, while making preparations to go out of the country, I switched some key weekends with my ex. It is very important to me that he will not know that I'm out of the country. It would be very dangerous for me but I also know that God is in total control and all is well. I always try to switch weekends in a way that the kids are with my mom, and it gives me peace to know that he does not have them.

Not this time. It's hard to put into words, but I will try. God gave me something; God never lets anything blindside you when you are on your face and behind the veil in a relationship with the Lord. This "something" is communion with Him and the enemy cannot interfere. That "something" is a type of communication that guides you and lets you in on what He is doing. I knew when I was rearranging the calendar that God wanted me to "Let it go" but I didn't. I said, "I trust You, but I trust my calendar and my planning too." I also knew that as I planned my calendar God was planning to un-plan my calendar. I knew He was going to undo what I just did.

Now the omer of manna that I wanted to share with you. When our team said *that city's* name, I look up at God. I can see Him smiling. I get the slap. I work the calendar. I do my thing, and then God does HIS. I had a thought in my prayer time. "Lord, I know that you are sending me there to *that city,* but I'm coming to terms with that, it is taking a while, but I am there now. I want to pray for them. I want to serve them. I want to learn to love my neighbor. But there are some people in that city that may recognize me. How do I handle that?"

Well, last night my son comes home with the omer of manna for His mama. "Mom, dad doesn't want to switch that first weekend that you wanted too. It seems his sister and her family are coming in from *that city,* and they will only be in for a short time." You mean to tell me that the God of the Universe who has far bigger things than me to worry about can orchestrate the universe so that his sister who has not been in the U.S. the whole time I was married for six years, and divorced for fourteen years, is going to put things in motion in a way that the very people that could recognize me in *that city* will actually be in here while I'm actually in *that city*! Yes, that is a wordy sentence. It is big, people! In case you missed it, that's twenty years, people! AWE. These are the days of AWE!

Looking back, I had to let it go. God is freedom! My omer of manna represents the fact that I have come to trust the Lord, and not a man, for everything I need. He is freeing me from the bondage of worry and fear. My experience during my time in the wilderness has brought me to a place where I know without a shadow of a doubt that my God shall supply all of my needs according to His riches in glory. He is freeing me from leaning on the arms of flesh. I can trust Him that He will take care of my kids when I am away. I can trust Him that He will take care of me too. He is an awesome, Everlasting Father who loves us!

Now the LORD said to Moses, "Come up to Me on the mountain and remain there, and I will give you the stone tablets with the law and the commandment which I have written for their instruction."

Exodus 24:12 (NASB)

Now on the next day Moses went into the tent of the testimony; and behold, the rod of Aaron for the house of Levi had sprouted and put forth buds and produced blossoms, and it bore ripe almonds. Moses then brought out all the rods from the presence of the LORD to all the sons of Israel; and they looked, and each man took his rod. But the LORD said to Moses, "Put back the rod of Aaron before the testimony to be kept as a sign against the rebels, that you may put an end to their grumbling against Me, so that they will not die."

Number 17:8-10 (NASB)

Then Moses said, "This is what the LORD has commanded, 'Let an omerful of it be kept throughout your generations, that they may see the bread that I fed you in the wilderness, when I brought you out of the land of Egypt."

Exodus 16:32-34 (NASB)

Pray for Target:

- Pray for radio listeners to understand the message and respond and for those who produce the programs to do so with clarity and simplicity. Pray for the finances to continue this broadcasting.
- Pray for those godly pastors who still minister in "Target" in spite of government repression, that they will preach the Word boldly, yet with wisdom from God.
- Pray for those in the "Target" country to be visited by the Holy Spirit in dreams and visions.
- Pray for the persecuted Persian believers to have endurance and to be able to show the love of Christ to those who oppress them.
- Pray for the reopening of the Bible providing source in "Target." What a blessing it would be to have the Scriptures readily available again in "Target."
- Pray that the new believers will learn to listen to God by reading the Word and applying it.
- Some believers do not have a fellowship to attend. Pray that they will get encouragement from radio broadcasts, Scripture portions, or other Christian literature.

Pray for the team:

- We have the itinerary for the "Target" part of the trip. Pray for opportunities to encounter people that God wishes us to encounter.
- Pray for unity.
- Pray for the ability to focus on doing what we need to do in preparation both physically and spiritually.

Father, help us to give our hearts fully to You to be usable. In Jesus' Name, I pray, Amen.

Because God wanted to make the unchanging nature of his purpose very clear to the heirs of what was promised, he

confirmed it with an oath. God did this so that, by two unchangeable things in which it is impossible for God to lie, we who have fled to take hold of the hope offered to us may be greatly encouraged. We have this hope as an anchor for the soul, firm and secure. It enters the inner sanctuary behind the curtain, where Jesus, who went before us, has entered on our behalf. He has become a high priest forever, in the order of Melchizedek.

Hebrews 6:17-20 (NIV)

There above the cover between the two cherubim that are over the ark of the testimony, I will meet with you and give you all my commands for the Israelites.

Exodus 25:22 (NIV)

"Come, follow me," Jesus said, "and I will make you fishers of men."

Mark 1:17 (NIV)

Shoeboxes, Heat, And Open Windows

Yesterday, I got to share with the team a little bit of what it is like for a Muslim to convert. In preparing, I prayed that God would give me a visual to show to help keep the ideas in mind when we see a similar item. As the time approached, I looked around my home for something Muslim and realized it wasn't there. None of it. All I could come up with from my previous lifestyle was a shoe box of pictures. I have not spoken to or heard from or had anything to do with the people in the photos from my shoebox in over fourteen years. The people in my shoebox are my family.

As I drove to the house yesterday, I was alone in my truck. I had my window down, music playing, and it was such a pretty day. Without realizing it, I had my hand out the window like a little kid. I was doing the wave thing with my hand, but my mind was somewhere else. It was hot, my air conditioner broke, and I suddenly became very aware of my hand.

If I hold it palm up like a traffic officer saying "stop" against the wind, I am causing friction, resistance. If I lay it flat, palm down, I am going into the wind draft but having no real effect because my hand is aerodynamically lined up. But if I ever so slightly move my fingers up then down, and do it again, my hand feels free like it is flying. I love the feeling of flying in the wind, submitting to its power but enjoying it instead of resisting it.

I pull into the parking lot and come to the conclusion that it is very hot. I am very hot. No air conditioning in your vehicle during the hottest summer in a long time makes you hot. I have been hot all summer. I stay hot. I started to complain and caught myself turning my whine to praise, 'Thank you God for open windows."

I reach over in the seat, pick up my shoebox of pictures, it shifts, the cover falls off, and I see some of the faces in my box, it catches me off guard. I love those faces. You may be wondering what any or all of this has to do with one another. I realized, when I saw the faces in the box that I am so blessed.

I get to sing and praise God, play with my hand out the window like a kid because I am set free in Christ Jesus. I am not resisting Him (Spirit-wind) with my palm up like a traffic officer. I am choosing not to live in resistance, friction, and conflict with God. I am also not choosing to be indifferent in life by keeping my hand down. I want to live in His flow. This trip is a testament and witness to the fact that I am in a place that I am willing to go with His flow, even if his flow takes me to an uncomfortable place. He alone has cleaned out my "stuff" the old stuff, the Muslim stuff. He has made me new, and it is joyful. He has turned my whine into praise, my water into wine. Thank you, God, for open windows!

I have to go now; I can't focus. Mr. Richard is singing. Pray for me!

Looking back, I had been inconvenienced all summer with no air conditioning. God taught me that when life turns up the heat, roll down your window. This trip will possibly and probably be inconvenient. I won't get my way. I won't be able to have it my way. I won't be able to go out of my way to get my way. I can learn to live inconvenienced if it means I get to live in Him. This trip is an open window so that the people we encounter won't be like the faces in my box; who are unsaved, and unbelievers.

But seek first His kingdom and His righteousness, and all these things will be added to you. So do not worry about tomorrow; for tomorrow will care for itself. Each day has enough trouble of its own.

Matthew 6:33-34 (NASB)

Tenth Prayer Update

Prayer for Target:

- Pray for a massive people movement among the 5,000,000 tribal people of southwest
"Target" with many coming to trust in Christ.
- Pray that some living outside of "Target" who have come to Christ might desire to return to reach their relatives, as well as reach out to others. Includeing visits, or returning permanently to "Target." Pray that they might be bold in proclaiming their faith in Jesus Christ.
- Pray that President of "Target" and others in the Islamic "Target" government will lead the country with wisdom. The Bible tells us to pray for those in authority so that Christian believers may lead peaceful and quiet lives in all godliness and holiness.
- Pray that believers will stand firm in their walk with God at home, work, and school and be able to testify wisely about their faith in Jesus Christ.
- Along the Caspian Sea live almost 3,000,000 people who have yet to hear the Gospel. Pray for someone to reach out to these people.

Prayer for and praise from the team:

- Praise, we have our tourist number, and the visas are being processed in Washington DC.
- Pray for them to be accepted and returned to us promptly.
- Pray for unity.
- Pray for focus on God, His peace, provision, authority, and Word.

Prayer for personal needs:

- For my son, who is struggling to grasp why I am going and where I am going. He is very worried, and he needs peace.

- For my daughter who is so strong, she won't admit she is worried, but I can tell by her silence that she doesn't know what to do with all of this.
- For my children to be blessed and be a blessing while I'm gone. They have peace and trust in the Lord.
- For me, I know that people are praying because I know God is in control. I have peace that is so assuring. I am in awe of God's work that He alone is doing.
- 16 days until "Target" 39 days until Israel.

Father, help with the details and the things that come up, help us to focus on You and not the details and the things that come up. I pray this in Jesus name, Amen.

As for you, you meant evil against me, but God meant it for good in order to bring about this present result, to preserve many people alive.

Genesis 50:20 (NASB)

Love the Lord your God with all your heart and with all your soul and with all your strength.

Deuteronomy 6:5 (NIV)

The Lord your God is with you, he is mighty to save. He will take great delight in you, he will quiet you with his love, he will rejoice over you with singing.

Zephaniah 3:17 (NIV)

He answered: "'Love the Lord your God with all your heart and with all your soul and with all your strength and with all your mind'; and, 'Love your neighbor as yourself.'"

Luke 10:27 (NIV)

Finally, brothers, pray for us that the message of the Lord may spread rapidly and be honored, just as it was with you. And pray that we may be delivered from wicked and evil men, for not everyone has faith. But the Lord is faithful, and he will strengthen and protect you from the evil one. We have

confidence in the Lord that you are doing and will continue to do the things we command. May the Lord direct your hearts into God's love and Christ's perseverance.

2 Thessalonians 3:1-5 (NIV)

Pierced

Friday I took my daughter to get her ears pierced. We went to the mall. We never go to the mall unless there is a purpose or goal. I have never been a "window shopper." But we went, we explored, and in one shop she wondered into, we met a girl about twenty-three years old from the "Target" country. We talked, I told her where I was going (didn't give dates or details) and we had a nice conversation. Later, maybe thirty minutes, we ran into a girl working in a shop who is from Israel. She was also about twenty-three. We started talking, talked about past trips, and our love of Israel. We talked about who she is and her soon trip to see her sister's wedding. We talked about my trip. We figure out that we may be there at the same time. We exchanged emails, and after a wonderful, long conversation about everything, we parted with hugs. Her name is Ruth.

Later that night when I was praying I asked God why or for what reason did I meet these two very different, but, much the same young ladies? Both are unsaved. He revealed my heart to me. Even after all this time, I am guarded and reserved around Muslims, but open and enjoy my Israeli friends. It brought me to repentance of who I am and what I am doing soon. God needed to show me that I have not fully cleaned out my heart's attitudes. Without realizing it, I was still holding back on sharing Him.

It took me a moment to see that He needed to get me to this place of repentance now, to be usable in a couple of days. By God's grace we are like that to others we encounter in our day, it is easy to love on those we love on, but God grows us up when we learn to love those that we honestly don't want too.

God is love!

1 John 4:16 (NASB)

I needed to make a trip to the dentist. Before the dentist, I have to go to the pharmacy to get antibiotics to take. I have a heart murmur that requires this. I have a heart condition, people! When I got to the pharmacy, both people behind the counter were Persians.

Instead of being in a hurry, he asked if he needed to tell me about my medications, and I said sure. Learning to talk, listen, and take time with someone is such a gift that we as believers don't use enough. Too cool. I can be teachable!

Well, the receptionist at the dental office purposely did not schedule anyone before or after me to give me time with my dental hygienist. My hygienist commented that it surprised her that we had so much time to talk. I also took the whole office banana bread and brownies so that it didn't look like I was targeting only her with a gift. We talked about everything. God is good. She gladly took the Bible I brought that was in Persian and even said as she took it that she will read it to her grandson. She showed everyone and everyone kept coming around to hear what we were saying. All of the other staff are believers and want to minister to her. Their curiosity is hilarious! They peak around corners, whisper behind the half wall. Too funny.

She has not been back to Persia since1971. We discussed places, events, food, and she plans to show me how to make the chicken with the walnuts and pomegranate and get my Persian up to par. She also told me where to get Persian spices in my area. God was so amazing. His timing is so perfect.

Her daughter has recently gotten divorced while pregnant and is worried about the future, and we talked a lot about that. See how God is so good and allows you to go through something to find Him. Then He allows you to heal and then hopefully walk someone through the same thing. Then with all that He is busy doing, He still takes the time to organize events so that you minister when He wants you to at the most opportune moment.

Looking back, I still am amazed at a God that is so Sovereign and Loving! This family is so in need of Jesus! They are such sweet people. She asked about my dad, and I explained. She said that her father passed away two years ago and that he had also become a Christian. She is so open to the Lord. The timing is so perfect for now to get to know her family more. I would not have been ready for this months ago, but in His timing, He prepares everyone for their individual parts of His big story. They are practicing Zoroastrianism. Which means they believe in a whole lot of "nothing eternal." The good thing is "nothing" is impossible with God! Especially the eternal!

Please keep praying for her and her family. I will have to get a crown, but I've never been more excited! That means more visits to the dentist, people! More chances to share Jesus!

But He was pierced through for our transgressions, He was crushed for our iniquities; the chastening for our well-being fell upon Him, and by His scourging, we are healed.

Isaiah 53:5 (NASB)

Tide

I ran an errand at lunch today. Just completing this task that has been on my "to do list" feels like a huge victory. I purchased individual packets of Tide laundry soap, whew! I know you don't think, "Man that's fantastic, way to complete a task!" But then you have not seen my list. My list has included a lot of things, and I have added to my list and marked things off my list. But that little task of taking a trip out of my normal traveling path has stayed right on top of the list. It reminds me that I cannot say that I have accomplished anything until I purchase the Tide. In fact, several times I have completed the whole page except for that item. I have had to carry it over to a new list.

But now we are eight days out. Eight is new beginnings in Hebrew. The "tide" has turned. Today is the day to do that small and insignificant task.

Yes, I'm still looney, but God is teaching me that in the big and the small things, including *travel size* things, He wants to be a part of my process. This past week I handed Him everything. This past Wednesday night I cried out to God until 3 am about everything. I cried for a whole lot that I won't go into, but I got to that place that I let it all out, handed Him *my list* and repented of wanting *my list* to be completed. I surrendered my list and submitted to doing what He put on the list for the next few days. Well, nothing is impossible with God (Luke 1:37). He painted, He ministered, He participated, He worked, and He did it all. He did it better than I ever could. I sat back in awe on Sunday morning when I just put the last drop of paint on the second churches' painting project. I crashed Sunday afternoon, but when I woke up three hours later, I knew that I had no right to claim anything. He did it because I wasn't strong enough to do it on my own. Obviously, people! I had to take a three-hour nap!

But I'm finding out that it is not necessarily the act of completing a task on the list that is important, but learning, changing and growing during the process is. Did I consult God before I made the list? Did I ask Him what to put on the list? Did I make Him a part of the list? What were my motives, my desires, my interest, etc.? Did I make Him a part of the process of completing the things on the list? Did I glorify Him when I completed something on the list? Am I willing to admit what is *mine* and what is *His* on the list? Am I willing to repent and take off or change something on my list? These are just some of the questions that come to mind.

Looking back, I had to sit down, make a list, and learn to evaluate my list spiritually. I ask the hard questions. Am I doing this task because God said to or because it will bring me fame? Am I doing the task to make my life easier, or am I keeping up with the Jones'? So many things, but each one is important to God. Sometimes it takes the simplest task like purchasing Tide travel packs or taking a trip which is very much out of your way to remind you to stop and focus on Him. There is a victory when you focus on Him!

And His voice shook the earth then, but now He has promised, saying, "Yet once more I will shake not only the earth, but also the heaven." This expression, "Yet once more," denotes the removing of those things which cannot be shaken may remain. Therefore, since we receive a kingdom which cannot be shaken, let us show gratitude, by which we may offer to God an acceptable service with reverence and awe; for our God is a consuming fire."

Hebrews 12:26-29 (NASB)

Eleventh Prayer Update

Prayer for Target:

- Pray for the people that we will meet in "Target" and "Walmart" that we be receptive to the Holy Spirit's leading and for us to be available to be used to speak with them.
- Pray for the people to know the Lord and that their hearts be prepared in advance.
- Pray for the Holy Spirit to move in mighty ways.
- Pray for the other teams that are in a couple of days before us and after us.

Prayer for the team:

- Pray that we be usable vessels for His glory!
- Pray that we are focused on our preparations and that we make our heart preparations priority.
- Pray for good health, and safety to and from our destinations.
- Pray for our families left behind.
- Praise in advance. God is moving. God is good. Thank you, God, for being our Everlasting Father, and Prince of Peace!
- Pray for "Walmart" and gift delivery.

Father God, this is it. I pray I don't fail You. I know You won't fail me. You are faithful! Thanks for loving me and thanks for Jesus! In Jesus' Name, I pray, Amen.

Personal note, thank you, dear ones for your prayers. I have joy and not fear. He has given me a quiet confidence because He has promised to be with me each step of the way. He is a good and loving God! Pray for my children and mother while I'm away! This will be my last note before we go. Shalom!

Your word is a lamp to my feet and a light for my path.

Psalm 119:105 (NIV)

Humble

To be humble means to have a feeling of insignificance, inferiority, and subservience. It is sobering when you are writing a book, and you want to "tell" others about what God has done yet you have to use your "Find and Replace" command to eliminate the words that can show the reader where you have been. I am humbled by the very character of God in that He took us to a dangerous place, and He brought us back again. It is still so dangerous that I cannot type the countries' name.

Now a new and interesting problem. How do I tell you without telling you what went on? For security reasons, I simply can't share too much. I start to type and tell you about our first steps into "Target" and my paragraph looks like this. Have fun guessing, people! We got off of the ******, and we were immediately sorted and told to go to a line for "non-Target" visas. We were questioned, fingerprinted, and processed. We were able to retrieve our **** that contained our *********. We planned to give them to ****** and *******. We stuck together as a group from *******. We came down the escalator that was already shut off because the ********* had only one or two ******** in a day. We proceeded to the security sections to get our ********* processed before leaving the building. No one was at the security station. So we put our *************** on carts to go through the main door. We are shocked, and ********* cannot believe the blessings that we have just walked past security.

But then I hear someone saying, "Come back, come back. You must go through the security." I explained that no one was there. "Ok, ok, please, come." So we followed the guard and returned to the position at the beginning of the x-ray machine. The man disappears and then returns, and is fussing in Persian to the lower ranking man. ********* asks what is happening. Remember he has not been a ********** for very long so his language skills are in their learning stage. But ********* has a great love for the Lord and a love for the people of "Target." To me, ********** has all ******* needs to do the Father's work.

My friend ********** asks me what they are saying. The high ranking officer is totally yelling at the low ranking man for leaving his post. The low ranking man thought that the ******** was over and that he could take a cigarette break. They did all of this as they shoved our ********** through the x-ray machines. I don't think that they ever even glanced at the screen. My friend ********* kept asking what they were saying and I said, "Say a prayer and give the Lord praise, and let's get out of here." Someone said, "Let's go exchange money." Me and the leader both said, "No!" at the same time. We were like-minded. Let's go!

We were thanked for returning to the security area, and we then moved outside of the ******* to meet our guide. We load up our *******, and we get into the van. I am as high as a kite on GOD. You should have seen what, "He hath just done, people! (SNV)

We are not home free yet. Hardly. We are loaded up, and the driver turns onto the highway. Let the adventure begin I thought. "Where do you want to go?" the lady guide asks. How about to ********** ********** tomb. It is a great start to your trip. "Sure, why not!" I'm pretty sure everyone on our team was freaking out. They looked a lot like Adam before getting on the roller coaster. But I was willing and sitting up front, and she asked me directly. So we went.

We had to go through security and then we went inside. We were in a very holy place for the people of "Target." Seriously, I wish I could tell you, who's grave!. You would die, people! Come and hear me speak sometime and I will verbally tell you! After a body search, of course, can't be too careful!

But we wondered around the "complex." It was a place of worship, and people are praying. I should not be allowed in these places. I defile them by my very being. I am dead to the Muslim world. Dead I tell ya! So I am walking and defiling, and our guide explains this or that. Then it dawns on me that I am having another one of those cross-cultural moments that makes me laugh. I am a divorced former Muslim who is walking through a ********** and defiling every bit of the *******. I should be nowhere near this place! I still can't decide if that is one step up from former

Muslim that became a Christian that played a Jewish dancing girl in the Passion Play. Hmm.

There are little areas of alcoves and domes. I hum "Jesus loves me this I know." Some of my team members shush me, and others giggle. Some join in. We prayer walk. The people of "Target" pray. We prayer walk. The people of "Target" hold their babies up to touch the screen around the tomb to get a blessing. We prayer walk. The people of "Target" put money on the tomb asking for blessings for this and that. We prayer walk and our hearts break...*don't they know Lord? This man can never bring them what they ask. He is dead! You are alive! You are the real deal. You are the very thing they need.*

There are racks of holy literature, and we slip a couple of good gifts of bread in the racks. Prayerfully someone will find them one day. I ask if I can take one of the prayer stones for a souvenir. Shiite Muslims place the clay-stone before them when they pray. The guide and the "complex" guide like that question. One asks, "Why?" So I can remember this place in my prayers." They grin and say, "Yes, yes." I have no idea why I just did that. I don't like that stuff anymore.

We get back in our van and off we go to tour "Target." We pull into our hotel, and the employee comes to get our bags. Per our training we let the men of the trip do all of the leadership, checking in, etc. to conform to the customs of the country of "Target." We also have to wear head scarves to conform to the customs of the country. Yeah, us. I hear the two young men comment how heavy our bags are. One asks the other, "Are they just starting their tour? Their bags feel so heavy like when someone shops too much at the end of the tour." Uh oh. I go over to the team leader and tell him to give the two men really big tips and pretend you don't know that the amount you are giving them is very large. Then I said, I would explain why later. He does it, and it works. A good tip always erases the memory of back muscles. I told our leader later, and he laughed. Good thinking. Good God, I thought! He is so good!

So I can't explain too much of where we went or what we did. We toured and became like "Bond, James Bond." We saw sites that are of Biblical proportions. Seriously, graves of the greatest kings of man. Sites that set the course of history for the Jewish people, "For such a time as this." We saw Biblical manuscripts by touring old ************ monasteries. I love hand-painted, handmade paper with calligraphy. We saw the greatest museums of the greatest jewels, rugs, artifacts, and history of the county of "Target," all the while fulfilling our Father's desires and bringing Him in by prayer and petition with thanksgiving and **********.

Some of my favorite moments purposely appear out of order so that they won't be trackable. One man in "Walmart" cut another team member and me off in a security line. My team member looked up and almost fussed, "he cut in line." But just as they were about to speak the guard noticed the man and zoomed in on him. He put that pushy man through the ringer. He went back and forth through the x-ray, eliminating gold watch, then coins, then this and that. We got motioned through and they never even checked our stuff. Blinded by Lord, people!

Our lady guide had to leave us unexpectedly because something happened (can't give details) and she would no longer be able to tour with us. We said our goodbyes and asked if we could pray for her. She said yes and we did. God is good.

The next morning I came down to the lobby. We were going to travel today to a new city. As I came to the lobby desk, I needed to get my passport back. Yes, every time we returned to the hotel, we had to surrender our passports. Trust and obey, people! The new guide made a flirty comment to the man behind the desk. He put his head down blushing and whispered, "I think she understands Persian." The new guy then says, "So, no way she heard that." I then greeted our new red-faced, couldn't get an apology out fast enough tour guide with a nice hello and "yes, I heard you." I walked away grinning like the cat from Alice. Poor guy, I have such a naughty streak in me. I just know that is why Christianity was so appealing. It was the only faith that explained my naughty condition. Original sin, so that's what they call it, people!

We move on, and one of our next stops is a carpet shop. Ok. We are game. I don't want one, but I will look. I love everything about the place. Seven of us plus our guide go in. The salesmen lower the window blinds signaling to other buyers that an important customer has come to shop. Have you ever shopped for a Persian rug? Well, it's a treat! They serve you tea and sweets and try to figure out what you want to purchase. Once they know the color, size, and amount you might spend, then they go all out. They will lay out carpets so fast and flip and show and do it again. One of our team members decides that she is "interested." That's it; they zoom in on her. We all sit and drink tea.

Time passes, a lot of time. She is indecisive. The carpet workers are frustrated. Our guide comes over and asks me in Persian so that our team member cannot understand. "Is she single?" To which I reply, "Umm, yes." He then says, "I knew it; that is why she is because she takes too long to pick a husband and too long to pick a carpet!" I am laughing, and I translate it to the group. Too funny. This guide has a good sense of humor. Our team member finally caves and gives up, unable to make a decision. We leave the store. Now we have just totally insulted the carpet workers, and as we go out the door of the shop having bought nothing, our male guide says, "Let's go fast before they come after us!" Always an adventure.

We continue to tour and eat the best food and drink the best tea. One of the first nights there the whole team comes down with sinus infections. We are breathing air that is very polluted. Some of us go to the pharmacy where you can get antibiotics without a doctor's note. Not me! Me and ********* who is our in-country contact go to the local market and get Persian limes. Now they are not limes but a lime-looking sweet green fruit that tastes like a really good tangerine. They are loaded with vitamin C. We go back to the hotel with about a dozen each. During evening prayer time in our hotel room, he and I cut the fruit in quarters and suck the juice. It is a lot of work, and some of the others are not brave enough to do it, but it works. Our room looked like a frat party with lime shots. We are the first to recover. I love those things.

Another fun time was teaching the team to drink tea. The hosts serve small individual pots of tea on silver or glass trays. Each tray has sugar cubes or sugar disks to sweeten the tea. The in-country contact and I start off in the ritual of drinking tea while the others watch. First, you pour the tea into the glass that has a saucer, then put the candy sugar disk on your tongue. Pour the glass into the saucer to cool the tea, and drink it from the saucer over the sugar disk. It's awesome!

Here is one last tidbit because I can't give you too many details. All trip long I kept a straight face and taught one of our team members a Persian phrase. While I did this, I was cracking up the van driver, the local guide, and our tour guide. Three people from "Target" went with us everywhere we went. Our Father's work was done. Still in awe, people! Every time our guide asked what we would like to see. Next, I taught ******** to say, "I want to shop." What I really taught her was, "I am crazy." I later explained when she started to have doubts, probably because the three locals were giggling, that I was on the up and up. Well, I lovingly convinced her that the phrase was correct. I taught her to add in, "I want to really shop." She was convinced. She said it a lot. I loved it. Now, I have to confess; I taught her to say, "I am crazy. I am really crazy." But she didn't know. The last night of the trip we were in a local shopping area. She was so proud as she used her phrase on a local shopkeeper. You should have seen his face when she spoke. I can show you; I videoed it. I also used that moment to confess and repent of my sinful nature. I got the whole thing on video including the, "I'm going to kill you, Shahe!" It's all good, people! She still loves me.

Looking back, I wish I could tell you all of the wonderfulness that the Lord allowed us to join Him in what He was doing. It was such a trip of blessing! I got to eat food and fill my heart up with Persian everything and break my heart all at the same time. My heart has forever been pierced with a great love for the people of "Target." Our prayer warriors had specific times in advance to pray for intercession. I just love the body of Christ!

One other note. Whenever we went out to eat, because I was familiar with the food, we would place our order at the restaurants. Different people would order different things and sometimes they liked it and sometimes they didn't. Because I was familiar with it, others would see my plate and "want what I had." They even started saying, "I'll have what Shahe is having." I will explain this later in the book but don't forget! This is really good Persian food, people!

Do not be wise in your own eyes; fear the LORD and turn away from evil. It will be healing to your body and refreshment to your bones.

Proverbs 3:8 (NASB)

The Balcony

We have returned from "Target" and we are in "Walmart". "Walmart" is the home of *that city*. (Insert dramatic music here.) We spent several days here before our trip to "Target," and we will spend several days after the trip here in "Walmart." "Walmart" is so not my favorite place to be. They dress funny here. I seriously hope you get my humor. I am so sick and wrong. Sorry folks, I am me!

Walmart not a Persian country, but it is a very Muslim country. I would pretty much like to be anywhere but here. Seriously, Macy's, Nordstrom's, Dillard's, name a different store, people! But God knew that, and that's why when this trip was proposed it was proposed in a different way, and we were going to shop in "Kmart."

We have all slept a lot. Lots of days of going to bed very late and getting up very early has taken a toll on us. Oh, and throw in a big bunch of STRESS and a touch of James Bond. But it is morning, and I go out on the balcony of this place.

It is an extremely hot place. Over 120 degrees I was told. No grass, only sand in sight. This is not the woods or mountains that I love. This is a desert, and it is very hot. The balcony is made of some type of stone. It's made of the stone to help keep it cool, but I soon go inside to get some slippers because my feet are getting hot.

I dress in traditional clothing with the exception that I do not currently have my head scarf on. I venture over to the balcony railing that juts out farther from the building. I want a better view. We are a couple of stories up. I look out over this city.

As I stand there for just a few minutes, the sun begins to warm my skin. It is getting really hot. I am wearing a salwar chemise. Whew, I miss my t-shirts! I see palm trees and start to watch traffic. It was all so normal and not so normal at the same time.

132

If I had stayed married to who I was once married too, if I had stayed a Muslim, if I had… and the list goes on and on; I could have very well been standing on a balcony very much like this one in this city. I would be standing there in the warm sun wearing clothes like I used to wear, seeing palm trees and watching traffic.

That's when God's Glory came down. I felt it and melt in a single motion. I hit the marble-like stone floor. I remember it being cold on my cheek for a moment. But when God's glory hit me I also had a "God's perspective type of vision."

It's hard to write this accurately so, please bear with me. In the melting, I saw TWO different lives at the exact, same time.

The one on the left: if I had stayed married to who I was married to, and if I had stayed a Muslim, and if I had… and the list that goes on and on; I saw a lifetime pass before my eyes of events and people and places and the vision ended with me standing on a balcony just like this one dressed just like this in traditional clothes, including the palm trees and the traffic. But this side showed me that I was destined for eternal hell.

The one on the right: showed me my decision to divorce, to become a Christian, for my children to become Christians… and the list goes on and on; I saw my lifetime pass before my eyes of events and people and places and the vision ended with me standing on this very balcony dressed just like this in traditional clothes including the palm trees and the traffic. But this time, I was shown that I was destined for eternal life.

That was when the melting happened. It just did. I melted like I did in the courthouse when my children's custody was being decided, and God told me, "I told you, don't do it." During that balcony moment, God revealed to me my disobedience and its consequences, but He also revealed to me His great love for me. During this balcony moment, God revealed to me my obedience and its consequences, but He also revealed to me His great love for me. Overwhelming! Overwhelming and that's why I melted. God's glory is thick and wonderful, powerful and, unlike anything I have ever experience except on that other balcony. I double-dog dare you to stay standing! You can't! I can't! I didn't! I went down.

The whole time I was married, the whole time I was divorced, the whole time he has been remarried, and just a few days before we left for the trip, my ex-husband has insisted that we should move the children and us here to "Walmart" to live. Twenty years! Time just stood still, and I could feel my life coming to a complete circle.

I had a balcony moment that allowed me to see my life like God sees it, from a God-like perspective. I peeled myself off of the stones, and I just began to sob. I think I sobbed for hours. I don't even know how long, time just stood still

I sobbed because I am saved. I sobbed because I was on a balcony and I felt the glory of God fall on me so hard that I could not breathe. It is those kinds of moments that I just know that I know that I am loved by a Merciful God that pursued my heart until I could no longer resist Him. I praise God for His commitment to my soul!

I sobbed because I now know faces, I now have friends; I now know names of those that are just like me in "Target" and that pray to a god that claims to be "merciful and compassionate." I sob because of the deception. I sob because their faith has no ability to forgive sins and give eternal life. I keep thinking of the people that I saw, the people I was introduced to, and the children that I saw playing, the elderly couple that was begging for money, and the young girl that did not want to go home. One man even asked if one of our guys would like to marry his sister, she wants to go to college. There were the tour guides, the housekeepers, and the girl in the market. What about the family that invited me to come to their home and the taxi driver.

I forgot to tell you about him; he drove like a maniac, but we lived! We passed our hotel, and I said in Farsi, "We passed it, it's back there." He stops the car suddenly, put the shift in reverse and we back up in traffic in full reverse. Two of us were on the floor, and I held on for dear life as he spoke to me. I <u>loved</u> this man instantly. We were speaking in Persian. Mine was broken Persian because of the different dialects. I explained that my father was Persian, and my mother was American. He has three sons; I have two kids. He asked where my father was living, and I said that I currently did not know. He is not pleased with me right now. While driving he tells me, "Daughter if you were my daughter I would never stop speaking to you. I have always wanted a daughter." I gave him my personal Bible and hugged him goodbye in tears. I really needed to hear that. He really needed the Bible. God is good to both of us.

I sobbed because I wished I could do more. I want to go back and not be here on this balcony. It feels normal and not so normal to be here watching traffic. It's such a sobering place to be when you are still in a country as we are in and just off of the field and missing your babies all at the same time. I keep thinking more! More gifts, more conversations, more encounters, more planting, more Him, more, more, more. I felt like a helpless infant. Babies' first words are usually, mama, dada, no, more!

I fell asleep. Later, I choked down food because I could not swallow. My teammates let me be. They probably thought someone had taught me a new phrase, "I am crazy, I am really crazy!" But I knew better. This was a love bigger than my own heart could contain, and I am crazy to try and contain it!

Looking back, I just know that I know that I know that if you don't have Jesus, and you are reading this... You have got to get Him! Please don't wait! Please want more! Now below is what He spoke to me. It's not the normal end of a chapter verses. I have shared with you what He shared with me on that balcony.

Now when Jesus heard about John (the Baptist), He withdrew from there in a boat to a secluded place by Himself; and when the people heard of this, they followed Him on foot from the cities. When He went ashore, He saw a large crowd, and felt compassion for them and healed their sick.

Matthew 14:13-14 (NASB)

Before Jesus moves, before Jesus acts, He withdraws from this world to be alone with His Father. These people were looking for Him. They were seeking Him. They were responding to Him. He then heals them. To minister to them, their souls, their spirits, He must heal them first. He had to meet them at their place of need, their place of pain, their place of despair. If He did not do this, they would be unable to focus on Him. When their flesh needs were met then, they could focus on their spiritual needs. They can now focus on Him!

When it came evening, the disciples came to Him and said, "This place is desolate and the hour is already late; so send the crowds away, that they may go into the villages and buy food for themselves."

Matthew 14:15 (NASB)

Time. How often do we let time define our actions instead of Him who created time? We think or listen to others around us instead of the One who created us. Also, we rely on what we see with our natural eyes and our knowledge to decide how to best work out situations or circumstances. We think we can go to Him and tell Him how we think a "problem" should best be solved. When in actuality, we should sit in a quiet place and pray to Him. He models that at the beginning of the story. In our attempts to "solve" or "fix" or "manipulate" a situation, we forget to have His love, grace, compassion, and mercy. We see it as being easier to simply send a hungry person away to get food instead of providing if for them. We take the easy way out. Let each person feed himself or feed his own, that way we don't have to be bothered. Problem solved.

But Jesus said to them, "They do not need to go away; you give them something to eat!" They said to Him, "We have here only five loaves and two fish." And He said, "Bring them here to Me."

Matthew 14:16-18 (NASB)

But then Jesus replies, "They do not need to go away. You give them something to eat." Their "need" is not to be forgotten or sent away because they need to be fed. How often do we want our problems to just go away? He commands us, "You feed them." When He says to us "give them something to eat" it means two ways to feed them. Physically, the body need must eat to be healthy to live. Spiritually, the body must eat to be nourished, grow, and eternally live. It means it is harder but to "do" or "work" at feeding those that He commands us to feed is what He desires.

Who does He ask you to feed? Whose needs are you to be meeting? He doesn't say eat first and then feed the others, but feed His people that come to the place, and that wish to meet with Him. His purpose is to meet with them. He is the bread of life that nourishes those that seek Him and follow Him wherever He goes. Unbelief, doubt, control, our own ability, etc., all limit us. How He can work in us and through us is limited by us. If He commands it, then we should simply obey it. But that is too easy. Instead, we doubt ourselves.

Faith is when we see with His eyes, hear with His ears, touch with His hands, feel with His heart, and be in Him! We have only five loaves and two fish. How we doubt and limit Him. We define life by what we see (five and two), and what we know (five and two), and what we think will solve the situation (five and two), and what our hands can hold (five and two).

"Bring them here to me," He said. We can't feed them on what we have and what we know. We can't because we are limited. But He can. He can because He is limitless. All we have to do is to obey His command and bring them to Him. He will do the rest. He will feed them. He will be their nourishment.

Ordering the people to sit down on the grass, He took the loaves and the two fish, and looking up toward heaven, He blessed the food, and breaking the loaves He gave them to the disciples, and the disciples gave them to the crowds, and they all ate and were satisfied. They picked up what was left over of the broken pieces, twelve full baskets. There were about five thousand men who ate, besides women and children.

Matthew 14:19-21 (NASB)

And he directed the people to sit down on the grass. Taking the five loaves and the two fish and looking up to heaven, He gave thanks and broke the loaves. Then He gave them to the disciples, and the disciples gave them to the people. He wants us to be still, rest and sit a while. He wants us to take time and partake of Him.

He takes what God provides to us, looks to Heaven, aligns it with the Will and Plan of Heaven and thanks God for all that God provides us.

And in a posture of thankfulness, He breaks bread. Meaning once He knows God blesses it, He moves, He breaks, He shares, and He feeds. He first gives it to the disciples, the learners, because you must first learn before you can teach. He gives it to the disciples to have them share it with the crowd. They all ate and were satisfied, and the disciples picked up twelve basketfuls of broken pieces that were left over. His word, His bread, He satisfies. He is enough. That's all we need to live. He always has more to give.

Don't waste His word! Don't mistreat it. Respect it. Pick up the pieces, collect it because He is of great value! The number of those who ate was about five thousand men, besides women and children. How we don't realize how a small portion of Him can nourish so many. That's where the balcony and crying come back in. My guilt over not doing more. MORE. If I'm not careful, more could be more of me and not Him. More needs to be ONLY HIM. I wanted to do more but repented and, as He showed me these passages, He allowed me to see from His perspective just a glimpse of His hands. He will feed them. He will nourish them. He is what they need. His ways are not our ways and in His way, He can feed the ones who choose to follow Him.

Our job is to obey and to follow His lead. We are to bring them to Him. Hand out our fishes and loaves, in this case, our "gifts" and when we are limited He will multiply it (the Word) among the people. On our own or of our own ability, (five and two), but when directed by Him, following His lead and His command, we can do more than we could ever imagine or hope for like it says in Ephesians 3:20-21.

So in a few words, "feed His people, problem eternally solved." AMEN!

Nine Days Between

Nine days between. That's how long it was between getting home from "Target" and going to Israel in 2007. I came home. I slept and loved on my babies, got things caught up at work, and prepared to leave again. I am looking forward to Israel. I am still high on a mountain top from the trip to "Walmart" and "Target."

When I went to Israel the first time in 2005, God taught me about love and forgiveness. "I am my beloved and my beloved is mine." God sang to me and gave me a desire for a deeper walk with Him. That was the trip where I wore white to be baptized in the Jordan River. That was the trip that I went to Jerusalem and represented a redeemed one because of all the generations on my Muslim side that would never have come to the Jewish nation. It was amazing to make a pilgrimage there instead of to Mecca. That was the trip that I got my beloved ring and my five red strings at the Western Wall. I went to Israel in 2005 with only the thought of going to the Western Wall and being baptized in white.

Between the first and the second trip to Israel in 2006, God taught me a lot about the Temple and told me that He was going to make me a "drink offering." At the time I had no idea what this was. This is the trip that He allowed me to see more of Jerusalem and to go up on the Temple Mount which is where the threshing floor was that David bought. I got to stand up there and take a really good look around. I could see the Eastern Gate (Beautiful Gate) from a whole new perspective. I could also see how "off" the Islamic religion is. I stood there in awe of the Lord and His work. Because of Him, I stood there as an eternally saved person by the grace of the Lord Jesus Christ instead of as a Muslim visiting a mosque. This was the trip that God said that He was going to heal my lungs. This was also the trip that I got my Yeshua ring, my wedding band. I went to Israel in 2006 with only the thought of seeing more of Jerusalem and being healed.

Between the second trip and this trip to Israel in 2007, God has taught me about studying the Temple and the pieces in the Temple. He has specifically taught me about their meaning concerning prayer and intercessory prayer. I have also gone through another type of "threshing or sifting" phase in my life. The Lord decides for me to go on the mission trip and everything about this trip was a growing process, learning about unbelief and bringing illumination to a dark place. He illuminated the places in my life that I have left dark, as well.

When my family shut the door on me more than fourteen years ago, I, in a hurt position, shut a door, too. I stopped doing anything Muslim or Persian. I stopped doing and being anything that was who and what I was before the door shut. I did not eat Persian food, wear the clothes, or listen to the music. I let a hard place form in my heart. I let it harden.

Looking back, I saw the Bread of Life feed the hungry people of "Target." I wanted more for these people. But God showed me on a balcony that He is Enough. God softened my hard heart. I went to Israel this time in 2007 only with the thought that He must be about to teach me something because He has set this trip so close to the other one. I simply obey. I have no idea why I am going, but He is sending me. Today in children's worship we sang my favorite song to sing with the kids, "Our God is up to something good."

Behold, you will call a nation you do not know, and a nation which knows you not will run to you, because of the LORD your God, even the Holy One of Israel; for He has glorified you.

Isaiah 55:5 (NASB)

Israel 2007

From day one in Israel, the moment I handed my passport to the man behind the counter the adventure began. I was questioned and interrogated for around an hour in a back office. But it was different; I was different. I was made new, and I had confidence, not for myself, but for the first time, I was very confident in Him. I was so confident that He is enough that I just sat calmly and went through the process. Part of me giggled as I kept thinking, "If you only knew where I was for the last month!" But I decided to keep that to my newly confident self.

The Lord has shown me that I am not who I was. I do not have to be who I think I should be. I am who I am because of the "Great I Am." He has me in a place with my heritage, with my language, with my culture, and with my experiences all for a reason. My reason is to honor and glorify Him in all that I am and that I do. I need to share what He has done in me and not take any claim that I have accomplished or done anything on my own. I am simply His to own.

I traveled with my dear friend Requelle. We joined a group from Florida. From day one, I felt a part of the group. The first morning in Tel Aviv, everyone else was taking pictures with one another before getting on the bus. Robin came over to me and asked to take a picture with me. She didn't even know me, but she was true to her Jesus and herself. Robin just loved on me that trip. That's just the wonderfulness of who she is. She brings everyone into her family and loves them with all that is in her.

Each day on this trip we did some things that were different and some things that were the same as on one of the other trips. Each time that happened He gave me a unique and special "I love you, moment."

My precious, "peaceful" moment was in En Gedi. It is a place that I had been to twice before. I saw a small hydrax (rock rabbit), and I wanted to take a better picture of it. I followed the little one as he climbed along and around a very large rock. I got separated from the main group because I was busy taking pictures with my camera. You should not be surprised by that. I had found a family of rock rabbits, and I was enjoying taking their pictures and watching them.

Then two small Ibex female deer came near me, and I followed them with my camera. I followed their gentle footsteps up a set of rock stairs to a landing that I had never been to before. The next thing I knew when I looked up from my camera was that they had led me to a whole herd of Ibex. I was alone, I couldn't see or hear anyone from our group, and I was surrounded by 20-30 of the Ibex deer.

They were playing in the waterfall. The deer were eating, and two males were fighting and rearing up on their hind legs and butting heads. I watched them get tangled up with each other and take about eight minutes to get untangled. It was amazing! If I had wanted to, I could have reached out and touched one. I chose not to do it because I did not want to scare them. I stayed still, and they let me stay.

There was a very large male with huge curled horns that would just watch me. Eventually, I realized that I better get back with the group. I had been here a nice long while. I have no idea how long because peace transcends all understanding and time. And I wasn't wearing a watch. I wondered how to move and not scare the Ibex. I turned and looked at the male who was on a ledge just above and behind me. He watched me while I watched his family. I turned and looked a long time into his eyes. I nodded my head gently, and the big male nodded back to me. It was so peaceful and incredible. I have the best pictures.

My precious "strength in Him" moment was that I climbed Masada. The last two trips I have taken the cable car to the top. The last time I was here it was just after a season of being very sick with my lungs. God told me that He was going to "heal me." He is Faithful and True, and I return now to Israel not having had any major lung issues of any kind. This time, a group was climbing the snake path up, and I decided to join them. I fell behind because I was taking pictures. Big shocker! But Dr. Bob and Steve stayed back with me. Dr. Bob made me take two puffs of my inhaler, and we slowly climbed. I got dizzy from the medicine and had to sit a minute. Steve told me to zig zag up the path which was a military hiking skill.

I kept going, and as I prayed and talked to God, I began to remember. I remember how to turn everything around to being every step, and every breath belongs to the Lord. I remembered what He has done for me. My pace picks up, my breathing is calmed; I am no longer dizzy and the Lord, Dr. Bob, Steve, and I made it up Masada. Dr. Bob and Steve were awesome! I would go on to climb everything in Israel. I got pictures of everything too! I kept thinking of the verse "come let's go up to the mountain, let's go up to the Lord."

When we came down the other side of Masada, we took camels off to a desert place where they had tents set up, and we had a lovely meal. My roommate Kim and I rode a camel and drank Bedouin tea.

We went to Mount Carmel where Elijah prayed, and the fire came down from Heaven. On the hike up the mountain, I got ahead of the group. It can happen, people! I have changed! I also had my camera down! Near the top I urged the other hikers on, "Hurry, there are camels up here!" Some of them did hurry up only to whack me when I showed them a discarded pack of Camel cigarettes on the side of the path. That was the beginning of many a payback to come.

We stopped at a new place where they had Israeli tanks. The military guys wanted to get out and see them. We took a picture of all of the guys and girls that had served in the US Armed Forces and Eli, our bus driver, and Naphtali, our guide, who served in the Israeli military. They even asked me to be in the picture. I sat on top of an Israeli tank, people!

My precious "wet" moment happened on November 5th. I prayed about getting baptized again in the Jordan. I don't want to be a tourist. The morning we were to be baptized, I woke up and went down to breakfast knowing that the baptism was at the end of this day. I heard someone say that it was November 5, 2007. You have to understand, I have lost all track of dates and times. I just show up and say, "Here I am Lord, send me!" Really, November

5th? I was baptized as a believer in my home church on November 5th, 1995. It was twelve years ago today. I decide to be baptized.

Just before we do, Rabbi Baruch goes into a wonderful teaching about two reasons to be immersed in baptism. One reason is obedience, and the other is to signify change. Well, this year has been very much all about obedience and change. I get baptized, and when I came up, I threw my prayer rock from the Shite "complex" in "Target" to the other side of the Jordan River. Gone! No more stones in my heart!

My precious "blessing" moment happened one night when our leader asked everyone to dress up nice. We headed off to a secret location which turned out to be Cana. Cana a new place for me. We went to the place where Jesus changed the water to wine at a wedding. I walked into a very old church and saw a very modern painting made up of three canvases which had six water jars on them. It was the exact colors for the painting that I completed right before leaving for "Target." That painting had three water vessels and 2 Timothy 2:21 on it. Rabbi Baruch spoke and Naphtali, who is from the tribe of Levi and the priestly lineage, prayed over our group in Hebrew. He just happened to be on a landing, one step above the rest of us as he raised his hands and prayed.

It is just incredible to be a blessed part of God's family and part of His plan. The Lord showed me that this season of who I am is changing, He has made my water change to wine, and I've completed what He wanted of me for the drink offering. He has completed in five weeks and sealed off the past. He has forgiven and set free my future. He is going to give me a new song and new wine. I am to be a purified vessel to honor Him, set apart and useful to the Master, and prepared for every good work.

Our group was made up of wonderful couples from Florida. Most of them were military families. After Naphtali had blessed us, they handed out red roses, and the couples renewed their wedding vows. I went around the room and captured pictures with each couple as they exchanged their private vows. The men had planned this part ahead of time. Some of them had brought their wives of many years' special gifts. It was wonderful to see couples like Pat and Robin, Shirley and Hal, Dr. Bob and Rita, Steve and

Amy, Gary and Jenny, and Kim and Tom renew the gift of marriage in such a special place! Water to wine! It's a miracle, people!

A precious "time with a friend" moment with Naphtali was an evening that we were able to sit and talk. We talked about everything including my recent trip to "Walmart" and to "Target." I even told him about a conversation that I had had with our male guide. The male "Target" guide and I were walking with the group through a bombed out area that had not been repaired on our way to see a Persian bath. We came up to a building that had half of it destroyed and the other half remained. It was surreal. Devastation and yet pictures hung on the wall, and unbroken China could be seen on a hutch. I had just gotten brave and told the male "Target" guide that I would soon be returning to Israel. We were then standing next to the place where that bomb landed that destroyed the area we were standing in. He stopped and said, "Aren't you afraid to go there? To Israel? Isn't it dangerous? It is so violent in Israel!" I just had to laugh because I was standing next to a bomb crater in "Target" and he thought it would be dangerous for me to go to Israel! It's all about perspective, people!

My precious "funny" moment was on one of the last days in Jerusalem. Our group was made up of lots of military folks, and we were always on time, and it was great! We had some extra time after lunch to shop. I had no desire to shop but knew the area. I asked Naphtali in front of the group if I could walk down to the Western Wall. It was not far, and I love to people watch. "Sure, go!" The military guy friends quickly objected, but Naphtali assured them that I would be just fine.

I felt so brave! I bought a watermelon popsicle and made my way through the streets of Jerusalem down some stairs and crossed over to the area. I had to finish my treat before going through the security area. They have the largest Mezuzah there. I took time, this time, to really see it. I made it through security and just took a really good look around. No worries, no pressures. I sit under a shade tree. A Jewish man came up and asked me if I would like to get some wine with him and talk. He introduces himself as Aram. I started to giggle. Would my Persian father just have a cow if he knew I was being asked out by a Jewish man at the Western Wall to get some wine?

I explained my laughter and that I did not drink wine. "Coffee then?" This guy was persistent. Sorry, but I don't drink coffee either. I'm not sure he believed me, but we talked for a long time. I told him my heart belong to my Jewish Jesus. You know, I was just thinking, this may be another one of those moments when my culture crosses and in the funniest way. An Orthodox Jewish man asking a former Muslim woman who is now a Christian who has just been to "Target," out to drink some wine at the Western Wall. I can't make this stuff up, people! Yeah, well, it's probably good that my poor dad is not talking to me. This would probably make him mad enough to stop talking to me!

After I had told the man that I don't drink, he offered coffee, and then cola. We had some funny exchanges. He said he had come to pray at the wall. I joked, "And to pick up American tourists." I said that I had come to pray and watch people. He said that is why he came to talk to me. He said that there was something about me, I had an attractive light. I think that he was trying to say that I had "that!" We talked for almost an hour after he realized that I was going nowhere with him. He had a story to tell. He was looking for something. I think he was looking for Him!

We talked more about "that" and when he went away I asked God, What's up with that?" I had come to the wall to watch and pray. Aram had come to the wall to pray, too. Only it must be lonely to talk to a wall because he needed to talk and to be heard. I later watched several Bar Mitzvahs. I watched families and people interacting with one another. How often are we surrounded by lots of people but no one takes the time to get to know us and to listen? We are all like Aram. We have a story to tell. We need to be heard. We have a desire to find that one thing that would complete us. Only he was looking for someone and not for The One. Pray for Aram and others like him! Thank you, Jesus, for teaching me to listen!

My precious "brave" moment in Galilee. The first morning in Galilee, I woke up early and went down by the water to sit and pray. Naphtali came down and bid me good morning and went off to swim in the Sea of Galilee. Oh, how I wished I could do that! I spent the whole day wishing for that. Why couldn't I? The only one stopping me was me. The next morning I woke up early and put my swimsuit and shoes on and took my towel and camera down to the water. My sweet roommate Kim joined me by the shore.

I swam out into the Sea of Galilee just before sunrise, and once I was farther out, I just floated on my back and watched the sunrise. I stayed out there in the water until the sun came up over the mountains and it's rays made a sunshine line toward me. The line grew as the sun went up and I decided to stay until the sun touched my toes. I stayed out there in the water until the sky was filled up with the sunshine. It was something that I had always wanted to do but fear and doubt kept me on the shore. Not anymore! And Kim was wonderful to take a picture of that moment for me! Captured! That moment of wonderful, joyful, peaceful touch of the sun, on my toes.

You can have that wonderful, joyful, peaceful touch of the sun with your toes in Galilee, too. Just touch the Son of God or, better yet, allow Him to touch you from your head to your toes. You don't even have to get wet, well unless you want to. And if you get wet by being baptized, don't forget the hairdryer!

My precious "flight back" moment was on the flight back to Atlanta. I sat next to a Jewish archaeologist that worked at the Megiddo site. She is on her way to California for a conference. We talk about everything. She practices kosher eating but not much else, and although she is very learned and has many degrees, she has little knowledge of the Lord. She is Jewish but unfamiliar with the God of the Jewish people! I shared my testimony with her. I told her where I had just been, and she asked a lot about Persepolis because she had always wanted to study it but it is not safe for her to go there.

I showed her pictures, and we talked about Islam, and we covered an amazing amount of history in a 13-hour flight. Please pray for her too! I have come out of this season of travel with a new appreciation for people, for their stories, for their faces, and for their souls. I appreciate so much of what the Lord has given me. I am very blessed. I live in abundance! I have several Bibles at home, freedom to worship, two healthy wonderful children, food and my needs are met, and I have a job that I love.

I returned home after almost two months of traveling. I have been cold ever since I have returned. I guess that happens when you have been in the Middle East for two months and when you get back, it's the end of November. I don't remember fall coming in, but I guess it is here. I'm not sure when Halloween happened and why Christmas decorations are everywhere, but I am pretty sure that we have not celebrated Thanksgiving yet.

We kind of skip over that one. You remember Thanksgiving. It is the holiday between costumes and candy and Santa and gifts. It's the one that started by thanking God for all that He has done. We don't do that much anymore. Now it is about sports games and big parties, black Friday shopping, and sales. My spirit quickens and I decide to make my family celebrate Thanksgiving to God all year long. That way we can't forget all that He has done for us.

I close out the "year of favor" 2007 with returning to work to find out that my home church that was cracking and allowing the enemy to have a foothold has progressed to a large rift. It's a huge rift. Now both sides are far apart. They are so far that they cannot reach out and touch one another. Reconciliation seems to have fallen in the large rift, and no one seems willing to go and find it. We are breaking the heart of God. I am so thankful to God that He taught me early in this year of favor to be silent. I have a direct word from the Lord not to choose a side. Jesus doesn't choose sides. Did you not read about the woman accused of adultery earlier in the book, people? Part of the division involves money. The staff is being laid off. Mr. Richard who was just six month shy of working at the church for twenty years has been laid off.

Looking back, my trip to Israel was a giant "I love you" from the Lord. He taught me how to listen to people and learn their names. Remember their faces and learn to pray for them. People are a gift from God. A life that He has created for a reason is a gift from God! We must prioritize our lives around valuing what God

148

values and learning to let go of what God does not want us to hold on to. And if He tells you, "Don't do it, no, or quiet" then you need to listen. He has a reason!

And don't worry, I did not forget. I remembered that I was going to tell you more about ordering food and others liking what they saw on my plate. What I had looked appealing to them. Well, it happened in Israel too. My friend Hal and his wife Shirley stood in line behind me as we ordered lunch. Shirley asked her husband what he was going to order. He said, "Whatever Shahe is ordering, it always looks so good." Well, the three of us had a great lunch together, and it was really good because all three of us have Jesus. He is the very thing that everyone sees that everyone wants and a desires, and yet most everyone has no idea how to ask for what they want. We need to be willing to help them place their order. One serving of Jesus please, better yet, make that a double-portion!

On the next day the large crowd who had come to the feast, when they heard that Jesus was coming to Jerusalem, took the branches of the palm trees and went out to meet Him, and began to shout, "Hosanna! Blessed is He who comes in the name of the LORD, even the King of Israel.

John 12:12-13 (NASB)

My children are happy that I am home, and they have made me promise to stay home in 2008. I promised not to travel internationally. It is January. My words will come back to bite me by the end of the year. With Mr. Richard gone, I am in a new place at work. I still have the same office, but his door is closed. It's really sad. It's really quiet. Seriously, it is REALLY quiet. A couple of pastors in another area of the church asked me to come and work for them. I prayed about it but feel that God wants me to stay where I am. I keep thinking, "Who will take care of the children?" I did not move. I didn't have too. Everything else around me would not quit moving.

More staff is laid off. More division is sown. More pride is flowing. It's as if Satan is throwing the lusts of the eyes, the lust of the flesh, and the lust of the boastful pride of life all around and each church member is picking it up and making it their own. It's sad to watch a church implode. When I first started working at the church back in 1998. One of the first meetings I was a part of which included the head pastor, included him saying that he wanted our churches' name to be known in all of the nation. The sad thing is, I sat there wondering when Jesus would be brought into that fame. He wasn't. The cross came off of our logo because we were trying to be epic or is that relevant, or was that one of the other catchy church phrases? I like something else.

And what does the LORD require of you but to do justice, to love kindness, and to walk humbly with your God?

Micah 6:8 (NASB)

Now we are here and "we" are in two. We have two sides, two opposing groups of people. I've told you before that two in Hebrew stands for "witness." But it can also stand for fellowship, union with Christ, and division. Don't miss that, division. We are becoming famous but not for the right reason. Not for Jesus.

I will spend the next ten months learning to balance work within the Biblical boundaries of proper submission and authority.

150

I have a most beneficial book to help me with that. No, it's not by some famous author. It's the Bible, people!

Time and time again, something would come my way. If my direct earthly authority said to do something I obeyed. Unless, it was directly against what the Bible said. I had one instance where I had prayed greatly about a particular subject. God showed me to do this. I was told that I could not do that simply because it pertained to Israel. Well, I did not know what to do so I talked to God. I asked Him to fix it, and He did. God fixed the situation, and I did not have to do anything. I also got to teach about Israel and the Jewish people. Did they forget that Jesus is Jewish? Anti-Semitism flows through churches; we just choose to ignore it and to sweep it under our pews.

The summer events that I love to do with the preschoolers and children are especially wonderful. God allows me to taste what it is like to completely lean on Him for these activities and to be in charge of teaching the children. I finally get what I had wanted all those years back when I went to work at the other church. It is very satisfying!

Speaking of the other church, you know some of the same problems that I had there with submission and authority and being asked to do something that I was not comfortable doing has come back around all these years later with my home church's division. I am now able to handle things better. I learned not to handle them but to hand them to God. I have grown up, people! Now, I didn't say taller, just up.

As fall approached, I was given a very real dream. It was in color, and it was with all of the faces of the children that I had been a part of their lives for twelve years. In the dream, I saw a lion and I "saw" danger thinking that lion was going to hurt the children. We were around a rectangular pool. I would wear myself out trying to keep the children safe from the lion until I got to where I was so exhausted and outnumbered by the ever-moving, ever-disobedient children who would not stay safe when I put them somewhere safe. I fell to the ground exhausted. I landed at the feet of the lion. I begged the lion not to harm the children. Harm? The Lion of Judah proceeded to tell me that He was the one watching over the

151

children and that He would keep them safe. I needed to learn to be still and know that He is God. It changed everything. I let go of my ministry. I handed it back to Him. It was always His, anyway.

During my quiet time, the Lord starts showing me something new. I spend the evening studying my Bible for a couple of hours. The house is quiet, and the kids are gone. I reach over and pick up a piece of paper and start writing down a list of things that I feel the Lord leading me to write. It is a list of things to fix, paint, or repair around the condo. I don't understand it, but I write it. I put the pen down and have this overwhelming, "You need to sell the condo." Wait, what?

Sell my home? No God, this can't be right. But He kept showing me that if I fix, paint, and repair the things on the list, I will sell my condo and move to an apartment near the kid's school until they graduate high school and that apartment complex had a leaf and something to do with oaks. Wait, what?

I argue for three days, but I come to the conclusion that He knows what He is doing and that I would have to obey. I invite my sweet friend Keely to come and look at my place. She is a realtor, and I want her advice and help. She walks around and tells me all kinds of things that I need to do to sell the place and get a higher price. It takes some time to complete the list but by the time I am done, and the sign goes up in the front, I am at peace with selling it. As long as I stick to the list, God will make it work. I cannot add or subtract from it; He has made that very clear!

I went looking for apartments after work one day near the kid's school. It had the name oak in it so I thought it was where we should be. I toured four of them, but I couldn't get past the lack of cleanliness and the old kitchens with dirty cabinets. I left so disappointed and cried out to God. Why do you want me to leave my clean place for a dirty place? I also have to be very careful with Aalia's cat allergy. The journey is hard, God. But in that time of crying He tells me to drive and I just do it. I wind around the highway and cross the bridge, and I come to an apartment complex that I have never seen before. I dry my eyes and drop in on the manager. She is pleased to see me and shows me a model.

It is wonderful and clean. I leave and tell the manager that I will be back shortly after I get the kids from school. We return and the kids like it. We can only afford the two-bedroom apartment, so Aalia and I will share a room. The kids and I were given three hundred dollars for our birthdays. We pray about it and use that money to put down as the 300.00 deposit on the apartment. I turn in the paperwork and the deposit money. I tell her that we will move in as soon as the house sells. She has lots of units available and tells me that she will save me one on the third floor that has never had a cat in it. I would never have gone looking for these apartments if I had not first obeyed by looking for the other apartment with the "oak." God is so good!

Also in this same time-period, my sweet Adam has his birthday, and my sweet sister-in-law has a brain aneurysm. We start making weekly trips a thousand miles away to help with the baby and take my mother back and forth. We spend the month between Adam's and Aalia's birthdays driving back and forth to my brother's home. At one point the kids joked, "What about no traveling?" And I had to remind them, "No international traveling!" We learn to make the most of our time in a car for a thousand miles there and a thousand miles back.

October has been rough in our children's department. Several of our children have had their father's pass away, and one of our Girls in Action teachers passed away from cancer. I keep thinking that I need to take her family a food basket, but I never got it done. Fall Fest is here. It is the easiest one I had ever organized, partly because it is much smaller since our church is splitting. But partly because I have lots of experience. I had learned to "run a good show." Is it just a "show?" Part of me wonders how much event-related activity at church impacts a person. I don't know that answer. I am glad that I know the One who does! I also think that God is very kind to me. We are juggling a lot with trips to my brother's house and getting prepared to sell our home.

That evening was especially sweet. All the kids kept coming up to me and giving me hugs and showing me their dress up clothes. Everything ran smooth, and we had plenty of candy. No fires to put out. It was wonderful. Clean up was smooth, and I went to bed that night loving everything about my job.

The next morning, I got up and went to work. I had a lot of stuff to put away. I spent most of the day doing that. One of our music guys comes down and asks if I can watch his two young boys while he plays the piano for the funeral in the worship center. I thought the break would be nice, and I just love those boys. I sat in the nursery and watched the brothers playing. I love my job crossed my mind again.

The second in command pastor comes to the nursery door. Weeks earlier our head pastor was asked to leave. Division comes from the enemy, people! Don't let him win! But we handed him our church long ago. This man comes around the corner and says, "Can I ask you a question?" I said yes, but then he sees the boys. "I'll come back," he says, and he walks away. What was that? It is about 5:30 pm. The whole preschool is dark except this room. Maybe that's how he found me so quickly; I was in the light. I am so perplexed by his actions that I look out the door and see him walk away and down the dark hall. He is on his cell phone. Odd, just odd. I return to watching the boys and sit in a rocking chair. "You are about to lose your job, trust Me." Wait, what?

I clearly hear the Lord say again, "You are about to lose your job, trust Me."

But I don't want to lose my job. I love my job. What about my kids? Where will I work? I go on and on and then I just stop. I tear up. I just love watching these brothers play. Children are a gift from God. These boys have tan, brown skin like my babies and big dark eyes with the most wonderful eyelashes. Their hair has soft curls, and there is such a preciousness about how Ben plays with his younger brother Josh. Sweetness. Pure sweetness. *But God what am I going to do?*

"Trust Me." I no longer take long periods of time to come around. This small whine session was less than a minute. Record time, people! But God has taught me so much and changed me so much. I recognize His voice. His is the only voice to listen to.

After the boys are picked up, I go off to look for this pastor. I find the pastor in his office. I surprise him. I think he must have forgotten his question. It's getting late, and I step into his office with a strange confidence. I know that he is about to lay me off. He proceeds to talk circles. I honestly have no idea what he is saying, I never do. I keep thinking that he is not following all of the HR rules. I have a degree in Management and Human Relations, and I keep thinking, this guy does not know what he is doing. He fumbles. I sit in confidence. Not a tear. I have been here before, but I am different. I don't need a window to stare out because I have Jesus to focus on. Part of me prays Lord, please don't let them accuse me of something awful like last time. I pray for protection. He fumbles some more and then finally spits it out. He says that I am laid off, and it's because of financial reasons. The church is struggling. I just sat there.

"What no response?" He is taken back by my stillness. "No." "You're ok with this?" "No, but I trust the Lord. He told me forty-five minutes ago that you were going to lay me off so He must have a plan." With that he says once more that I am too "mystical" and that he doesn't understand because no one else knew that I was losing my job. I said, "God did." I was dismissed, but before I left I asked when does this go into effect? He left that part out. He doesn't know how to do all of this. He responds with whenever you like, just come back and meet with me sometime next week and we will work out the details.

I go back to my office with the Lord as my strength, refuge, and shield. I call the kids and tell them that I am going to be late getting home. I asked if they are ok. I don't say anything. I just sit in my office; I am waiting for the pastor next door to go home so I could pack up my paintings and plants to leave without answering questions. I clean up my desk and look around. I go and get a cart to put my plants on to take to the car. These are special plants. Back in 1999, the church staff gave me a container garden with four or five small plants in it when my sweet Granny died. The plants have grown, and I've separated them numerous times. They are getting heavy, and there are a lot of them.

I clean up my office. Load up the plants and pictures. I take a good look around my office. I still love my job. But I love Jesus more. Before I turn off the lights for the last time, I say out loud the words that I have painted in black on the walls of my office. I love this verse.

Let everything that has breath praise the LORD. Praise the LORD!

Psalm 150:6 (NASB)

It is nighttime and dark outside. I'm glad that I had everything on this cart because I pushed it down the ramp and load up my truck. I have too many plants. Where am I going to put them? I put the cart back and put my keys in the downstairs desk and leave a voice mail telling him where I had put them. I punch out the exit door and take a deep breath. I remind myself not to forget what God said. "You are about to lose your job, trust Me." Well, I've just lost my job, so now I have to start trusting Him in a whole new way. I remember the dream with the lion, and I leave my ministry at the feet of the Lion of Judah.

I come home to my sweet babies that are not babies anymore. I get them off to bed without telling them what has happened. It can wait I thought. I go off to bed and finally let myself have a good cry. I have not told anyone yet but God. He is so good to me. I fall asleep and have another dream.

This time, the dream is very real. I am in a room with other people deciding my future. I have no input. I then get moved to a new place where I get told that I am in charge of food and clothes. I am placed in charge of the "storehouses." God tells me that He will provide for me out of the riches of the reservoir of His storehouse. I wake up remembering this very real dream.

I take the kids off to school and come home. There is now plenty of time to repair and work around the condo. I start by figuring out what do to do with all of these plants. My phone starts to ring, and it never stops. Three different people from the church HR team call me and apologize and say it was not supposed to be me but another woman. I tell them not to worry, and I tell them what God said to me.

I have confidence because God walked before me and told me what was about to happen and all I had to do was trust Him. I let each caller know that I am ok, I am trusting the Lord. I then get a call from one of the housekeepers. She was in the break room and overheard the man who let me go and my direct supervisor talking to the guy that was now in charge of children's worship. They were fussing at him because he was turning in his two-week notice. They were mad and said that they wished that he had talked to them because they let me go last night. They were angry. My sweet friend says to call and get my job back. I tell her the same thing that I told the HR team. I'm ok; God told me to trust Him.

Then my phone starts ringing in a very wrong way. It is church members. Gossip has started, and some from both of the divided sides are trying to get me to pick a side, going so far as to tell me to fight for my job. I told them the same thing I kept telling everyone else. "I'm ok, God told me this was going to happen and to trust Him." I also turn my phone off.

Sunday is interesting. Stuff that I had planned to do on Friday was not finished. I can see stuff unfolding, and it is not my place to fold it back. God was clear, and I need to keep clear boundaries. I subbed for a friend and taught her Sunday school class and then went home.

I spent the next weeks from the end of October until December applying to every job under the sun. I could not find full-time work anywhere. Now think about it. I lost my job at the end of October 2008 along with large numbers of people across the nation. The housing market was crashing, finances are all over the place, the news is non-stop, and circumstances seem really bad. I keep trying to find work, and no one comes to see the condo.

The time at home allows me to keep cleaning up and cleaning out. I go through everything that I have not had time in the past to clean up and clean out. The kids have grown older. I take boxes of children's books to a local children's outreach ministry. I put a sign on the corner and have a spot yard sale every

Thursday for a month. It helps me clean out that which we no longer need or outgrew. Whatever did not sell was donated. It did not come back in the house.

I open the mail, and there is a card in it with three hundred dollars cash. I just stare at it. It's just before Christmas and my mind wonders. The kid's see it, and we decide to pray about it. All three of us come to the conclusion that God knows something that we don't know, and we put the money away for a rainy day. We can go without.

Well, the rainy day wasn't exactly wet, but it was winter, and our heater died. I called a repair man. He came and looked at the unit and said that it would be $350.00. The kids and I look at each other. We all know what we are thinking. But the man says he only needs $99.00 now, and he will order the part and return. One of the kids says that God gave us only $300.00. Guess He came up short. Well, hardly. Before the repairman returned, we got another note in the mail. Also, unsigned with $50.00 cash. It is so good to be able to show your children that you can trust in the Lord!

Looking back, I wouldn't trade this year that did not look anything like a year of favor for anything. I don't want a do-over, though. I am not a saint, well actually I guess I am. Maybe I should say, I'm not a nut to repeat it. Yes, it was really hard. I had to give up lots of things that I loved including job security and potentially my families' home. But I love God more. He gave me so many ways to physically show my children, His guiding steps, and allow me to tell and show them how He worked this and that out. We turned in the papers and the deposit for the apartment, and we were approved before I lost my job. My house was on the market and prepared before I lost my job. I had a cat-free apartment waiting on my family on the third floor. It was a great incentive to clean up and clean out that which we did not need anymore and share with those less fortunate all that God had given us. The money from the pop-up yard sale provided for a future rental moving truck. I had time to spend taking care of the kids and getting my stuff at home done. I finished. Keely came back, and she could not believe all of the changes. I had time to do them. God orchestrated that!

I still could not find work. I have twelve weeks of severance. It lasts until the end of January 2009. You won't believe this, but most of all of this happened between August and December. We closed out December with Christmas presents under the tree. Three each plus chocolate oranges! My sister-in-law was recovering and to God be the glory! My nephew was six months old when this happened, and both families pitched in to help take care of him. We made lots of trips back and forth including to pick up my mom to take her to her younger brother's funeral. My Granny's sister, my great aunt Mary died as well. She was an amazing lady. Our truck and my mother's car broke down continuously but in everything with prayer and petition with thanksgiving present your requests to God and the peace of God which transcends all understanding will guard your hearts and minds in Christ Jesus. That is how the year that did not look anything like a year of favor ended. We were blessed, highly favored, and at peace!

Rejoice in the LORD always; again I will say rejoice! Let your gentle spirit be known to all men. The LORD is near. Be anxious for nothing, but in everything by prayer and supplication with thanksgiving let your requests be made known to God. And the peace of God, which surpasses all comprehension will guard your hearts and your minds in Christ Jesus.

Philippians 4:4-7 (NASB)

Yet those who wait for the LORD will gain new strength; they will mount up with wings like eagles, they will run and not get tired, they will walk and not become weary.

Isaiah 40:31 (NASB)

My beloved responded and said to me, 'Arise, my darling, my beautiful one, and come along. For behold, the winter is past, the rain is over and gone. The flowers have already appeared in the land; the time has arrived for pruning the vines, and the voice of the turtledove has been heard in our land. The fig tree has ripened its figs, and the vines in blossom have given forth

their fragrance. Arise, my darling, my beautiful one, and come along!'

Song of Solomon 2:10-14 (NASB)

The kids have started back to school. Aalia is a junior and Adam is a freshman. Where has time gone? I spend my days looking for work. I don't have a computer or the internet at home, so I go to friends' houses to apply for jobs. One of my friends tells me that I need to get on Facebook so that I can connect with others and get the word out that I am in need of a job. I will try anything. I couldn't even get a full-time job at a local restaurant. I filled out the application and waited in line for three hours; she dismissed me in 10 seconds. Wait, what? I asked her why. She told me that I wrote down that I was available twenty-four hours a day, seven days a week except Friday nights. I taught some wonderful middle schoolers on Friday nights at the local Arabic church. She said, "If you work here, you work on Friday nights."

I am getting frustrated and tired. I get on Facebook to try this thing. I also keep applying for jobs. I keep cleaning out. I keep organizing. I have a floor plan of the exact size of our new apartment. I can look around and plan what will and will not make it up three flights of stairs. I get to work dealing with "my stuff." I get to work dealing with trying to get work every time I turn on a computer. I have only been on Facebook for a week, but Facebook is getting annoying. I decide to come off of Facebook. How do I delete this thing?

What have my friends done to me? I am pretty sure they have tricked me onto Facebook. I am overwhelmed with "be my friend," requests for digital ornaments for a digital Christmas tree? In the words of my friend Rita, "What's up with that?" But then the coolest thing happens. It is one of those fantastic God-planned in His timing kind of things. I get contacted on Facebook by two people from my past. Way, way, way past. They are from my high school. They were always telling me about Jesus. You might remember them. It's John B. and Tim L.

I have often wondered about them. The last time that I saw John and Tim was at a park beach. I was pregnant with Aalia. So much has changed! She is a junior. I have a son. And all three of us have Jesus! After accepting Jesus as my Lord and Savior, I wondered when or how I would ever get to tell them that I have changed. I sent them both emails today. I guess it is worth staying connected on Facebook.

Days pass and I get a chance to talk with both of them and give them a great surprise. I love how God works! Sometimes in an instant and sometimes over many, many years. Either way, He gets the glory!

I have two weeks left of severance, and Mr. Richard calls me. He asks if I can come over to his house because he would like to talk to me. So I head off and find it odd that his wife Terri stays in the kitchen while we sit in the family room. He starts to say that he and others have made the Lifelines ministry a 501c-3 non-profit, and he has been praying about hiring me. He says that he was praying that if I got a job (any job) that he would know that he was not supposed to hire me. But if I did not get (any job, like that restaurant one) a job before my severance ran out, then he would know that he should hire me. Wait, what?

I throw a pillow at him and fuss at him because he was the reason I could not get a job anywhere! I was so mad at him that I forgot to say, "Thank you for the job." I guess God was laughing at me because Terri and Mr. Richard were. Here we go again!

I start to work for Mr. Richard and the Lifelines Ministry at the very beginning of February 2009. I need to tell you that Lifelines helps people with food and clothing and shares the Good News of the Gospel of Jesus Christ with each person that comes through the ministry doors. We also go into section-8 housing and provide a meal and teach Bible study to anyone who wants to attend. God showed me a very neat verse on the first day at a rough apartment complex.

Bring the whole tithe into the storehouse, so that there may be food in My house, and test Me now in this," says the LORD of hosts, "if I will not open for you the windows of heaven and pour out for you a blessing until it overflows.

Micah 3:10 (NASB)

Mr. Richard taught the lesson that day. I never told him about my dream. But God was so faithful to confirm to me that day that I was right where I was supposed to be. I even wrote it in my blue Bible. God is always watching, and if we are willing to be positioned to receive His blessings, He will open the storehouses!

A local church allowed us to have my office in their offices and keep the food and clothing downstairs. I loved working with Cathy, Terry, and Barry. I get a call from Joe whose wife was the Girls in Action teacher that passed away last October. He wants to come up and donate some clothing and shoes. We talk on the phone for almost two hours while I fold and stuff the Lifelines newsletter. I got off of the phone and thought to myself, "What a nice conversation." It's rare to have a conversation with someone that is all about God. I went back to folding newsletters.

My job was settling in, and the Lord allowed my phone to start ringing. In one week my condo was shown many times. One of them was early on a Saturday morning. The kids were not home, and I overslept. I fussed and grumbled and got out of bed half-awake but I managed to get out of there so the house could be shown. No easy task when your bed is a mattress on the floor, and you have to disguise it. The "bed" that was in my room was four shelves that I laid and stacked on the floor and covered with many, many blankets to make it look like a bed. I kept thinking that when the condo sells, I will get me a new bed. The kids had beds, but I planned to get them new beds too because they were outgrowing theirs.

I had nowhere to go, but I could not be home. I drove to McD's pick up some breakfast, and I returned home and parked in the cul de sac behind my condo. I ate breakfast as someone toured my home. God, why are we moving? I have a job now. It seems strange to go to a place that is twice what I pay here? I apologized for complaining about getting up so early on a Saturday morning. And I was thankful for breakfast.

The man that toured the house that morning bought my condo for full asking price. With all of the changes that I made in that condo, I was able to make a profit. I paid off my college student loan. I was thankful that my college loan was paid off before my child goes to college. I was debt free. For some reason, that was very important in my next step. I did not know why but I "trust Him." I was cleaned out and sorted. I had sweet friends help us move, and we used a real rental truck to move in one day. I know, right! That was a first, people! Richard H. makes a comment, "Is this all of your stuff?" God is good. I don't know why, but being "cleaned out" and set free from stuff was also important. Obedience even when it doesn't make sense is important! Don't forget Ruth, people! We moved to the third floor and started a new adventure in new beds!

Summer rolls around and I am making plans to head back North to see John B. and Tim L. for the first time in many a year. I will take my mom and my kids, and they will stay with my brother's family while I attend a week-long conference with Pastor John B. on how to witness to Muslims. I will be staying in the home of one of the organizers because the conference is a couple of hours away from my brother's house. The Lord tells me to ask people to pray for me while I am up there. He specifically tells me to ask Mr. Richard, Richard H., and Joe to pray intercessory prayers for me. I have no idea why God wanted these three men, but they all agree to pray.

John and I sit at the round table in front of the speaker's podium. When the room is dark, and the speaker is in the light, so are we. They start off by saying that we need to find "common ground" with our Muslim brothers and sisters. Wait, what? Our brothers and sisters are in Christ Jesus. They go on to cover other points including that it is ok to call God Allah. Wait, what? No way! I raise my hand. "So are you saying that the God of Islam and the God of the Bible are the same, and it's ok to call them both Allah?" "Yes," but before he can finish, I can't help myself. "Sir I'm sorry, but I used to be a Muslim, and there is simply no way that you should say that or teach others to believe that. The God that I pray to now, the God of the Bible is alive and is in no way, shape, or form the same God as Allah."

Needless to say, it was a rocky first day. But every time I would get bold and speak up, I would get a text from Mr. Richard, Richard H., or Joe and it would be a Scripture verse. Every verse was a direct hit; it was amazing. They are a thousand miles away and have no idea what is going on in that room, yet the Scripture is perfect. I am encouraged, and I speak up. We do this round and round dance from Monday to Tuesday and by Wednesday the conference people have pulled me aside, and they have told me to be quiet. They do not want me to raise my hand anymore or object. The old me would have run home. The new me stayed.

I stayed right in that light at that table in the front of a room full of about two hundred missionaries that have gathered from around the world and paid a great price to be there. I stayed right there to make sure that Jesus was a part of what they were teaching others to share about sharing to the Islamic nations. At one point, one of them got frustrated with me, and he blurted out, "Have you even been on the mission field in an Islamic country?"

Why yes, yes I have. That simple question gave me 30 minutes to tell about "Target" and what Bread of Life that we took in to be shared with the growing numbers of believers in "Target." I was able to give my personal testimony of how God and Allah are not the same. You say that and leave the Holy Spirit out and Jesus out, too! I also got to say that teaching these people to go pray in a mosque is wrong. These folks have no clue what they were teaching!

I also stayed right there because no one else in that room would say anything, not a one. No one stuck up for me, three believers in my home state were constantly praying! I had a boldness like only God Himself can do. At each break or meal, I was approached by the missionaries who would ask me direct questions about witnessing to Muslims and what the conference leaders were saying. Sometimes it was hard to be in the room. John and I would eat lunch outside with his sweet wife, Cindy.

It was hard to stay in the leader's home. I was beyond not welcomed. I made an excuse Thursday night to excuse myself and return to my brother's home. Yes, I did miss my children terribly, but I felt like I was sleeping at the enemy's and my heart was so overwhelmed with the false teachings, and I was exhausted.

I returned to my brother's house, and we spent some time with Amanda's family. The house was full of laughter and joy and children. Games were being played, and I got introduced to Amanda's sister's new fiancé. His name is Joe. He is a Christian. It was so neat to see him pay such loving attention to his future wife and her family. We had a great evening. I went to bed that night in the spare bedroom on an inflatable bed. I was so tired, and I started to cry. The whole conference made me feel very alone. I kept trying to remind myself that God is here, for the first time in a long time, I really needed a real hug. I uttered the words, "I want a Joe." I fell asleep thinking that it would be such a blessing to have someone like Diana's future husband that was so loving and fit right into her family. I must be tired. This never happens! Never say never!

Friday is yet another day of the muck being spewed. I could not wait to get out of there. I skipped the second half of the day. I drove back to my brothers and took the paddle boat out on the lake all by myself. I asked God to help me. Tomorrow is the last day of the conference. It is a half day, and these folks are returning home with a whole load of muck and not enough Jesus. I asked for them to be "bound" and restricted from being able to say that God is Allah and that they are the same. I prayed and asked God to tell people to tell the ones that they will be witnessing too to pick up their holy book and directly compare it with the Bible side-by-side. I asked for them to have to answer the questions that I asked for the missionaries to be brave enough to ask. I asked for God to be glorified in that room and no one else. I asked all of this in Jesus name!

Saturday has all of the conference goers gathered in a room that we were not in before. No tables, just chairs. A stage up front with a podium and a table. All of the speakers were in chairs on the stage. They started to do what they did each day which is to pray. Each day of the conference, instead of saying, "Dear Lord," or "Father God," or using another name of God they would start by saying, "Allah, we ask your blessing...." UGH! What a load of muck! But today, they said, "Lord we come before You..." Go GOD! (Not Allah!)

Then they got up there and spoke for a couple of minutes and then said that they were going to open up the mic so that if anyone in the audience can ask a question to anyone on the stage about anything that happened at the conference. Go GOD! One by one people came forward and asked the questions on their heart that had been sitting their pricking them because their spirits were not at peace with what was said. They were brave enough to ask the hard questions, and the people on stage had to answer them and the way it all worked out, the people on stage were unable to answer them except by glorifying God the Father, God the Son, and God the Holy Spirit! They couldn't help themselves. It was incredible! Go GOD again!

The icing on the cake was when someone asked the head muck-slinger a question. He did not have his Bible with him (big shocker!), and he came down the steps and asked to use mine. It was the blue beauty by the way. He brought it up on stage and held it up side by side with that other so-called holy book and said, "Tell your people to compare their book directly with the Bible." UGH! I can't make this stuff up, people! I am getting excited all over again just typing it! It was amazing. Go GOD! Go JESUS! Go HOLY SPIRIT!

I had prayed the day before for all of this including Isaiah 42. I prayed that God gets the glory and not Allah. I wept on that boat out in that water. It broke my heart that believers were being led astray. I prayed, how can I protect the glory of God?

I am the LORD, that is My name; I will not give My glory to another, nor My praise to graven images.

Isaiah 42:8 (NASB)

God does not share His glory with anyone! It was the best Saturday ever! I left that conference knowing that God was in control and that folks that heard today would be able to witness to others including Muslims in the powerful and mighty name of Jesus and no other!

I spent Sunday sharing with Pastor John B.'s church and then giving my testimony to the youth group that he led. Tim L.

and his sweet wife, Krista came out, and it was great to spend time with my brothers and sisters in Christ Jesus!

Looking back, I remember my family returned home thankful to be home. It's good to be home! Home is where God places you and where you place God. In your heart, people! The summer was spent working for Mr. Richard and spending time with the kids. Summer changed to fall. My baby girl is a high school senior, and my baby boy is a sophomore! UGH! I can't believe how fast time passes. Winter comes, and we have a quiet Christmas. God is so good! God told me during my yearly one week retreat into Him that "He was going to sing over me in the New Year." Wait, what does that mean?

Oh, and I forgot to mention something, rather someone. You remember the guy that kept coming around named Joe. Well, he would show up, drop off some clothes, we would have a nice regular conversation about God, and I would not hear from him again. A month would pass. I asked him to pray for my conference adventure, he would, I was thankful, it was all regular conversation about God, and I would not hear from him again. A month would pass, and I saw him at one of Lifelines ministries. We would serve, talk about God, and I would not hear from him again.

At one point, he was telling me that he was praying about moving to Florida. He has family there. He wanted to know if I would like to move into his home. He wasn't ready to sell it yet and did not feel the Lord's leading to selling it. I told him, no, he had three cats and he had the cats for a very long time. Aalia would never be able to stay in a cat home. So, he kept his home, visited Florida for long time periods. In between when he was home, we would have a conversation about what God was doing in our lives, and I would not hear from him again.

I never really thought romantically about any of this because it was never romantic conversations or situations. It was always in a ministry related event or location or over the phone. Joe was never inappropriate, and there was nothing to misconstrue. It was just friendship in Christ. I have lots of friends in Christ, and we mimic this very pattern. Life keeps you busy, but you have "connection" time, and you have conversations about what God is

168

doing in your lives. It is encouraging and then life gets in the way, and you have to wait a while before the next "connection."

Sometime after fall but before winter during one of those conversations with Joe, he just says, "God told me that I am going to marry you." Wait, what? Right! Marriage. I proceeded to give him the pigs don't fly speech and that he must be nuts because he and I pray to the same God, and God NEVER contradicts Himself. I laugh it off, tell him no, and he waits patiently.

Funny thing is we never really stopped the once a month let's eat, talk about God, God told me that I'm going to marry you, I tell him no, part as friends, and see you next month. We did this for a while. Even as I type, I can't remember when this process started; it was just part of my season at that time, and I never really paid attention to it or him. Joe is twenty years older than I am. There's no way, says the little girl inside of me. "Yuk!" I thought that guy is almost forty…wait…sixty…wait…I'm forty…wait…yuk! Didn't you read the first book? Don't forget the gold and the camels, people!

For My own sake, for My own sake, I will act; For how can My name be profaned? And My glory I will not give to another.

Isaiah 48:11 (NASB)

All of us like sheep have gone astray, each of us has turned to his own way; but the LORD has caused the iniquity of us all to fall on Him.

Isaiah 53:6 (NASB)

His watchmen are blind, all of them know nothing. All of them are mute dogs unable to bark, dreamers lying down, who love to slumber; and the dogs are greedy, they are not satisfied. And they are shepherds who have no understanding; they have all turned to their own way, each on to his unjust gain, to the last one. "Come," they say, "let us get wine, and let us drink heavily of strong drink; and tomorrow will be like today, only more so."

Isaiah 56:10-12 (NASB)

It seems funny to title a chapter by a number, but oh what a number this will become this year. We have had a quiet Christmas, and it is fun to watch the snow fall from a third-floor window. It is January, and I am not painting much. There isn't room here to do it, but it's ok because here has white carpet. And when your child is a senior in high school there isn't much time to do anything! I am busy with activities at the kid's school which is very close. I am busy at work, and a couple of new trips are in the works. Aalia and I will go with a group from her school to Greece and Italy in June. I have also signed up to tour Turkey and Greece with Rabbi Baruch's group. We plan to visit the seven churches in Revelation along with other significant Biblical sites.

I look forward to these trips abroad. It causes me to really study my Bible. I am now a major map reader, and I like learning about where I am going! I'm telling you, God is in the miracle business, people! During January, I am at a Bible study and one of the participants makes a funny comment and I am not sure what to do with it. I decide to do nothing. I will wait on the Lord. I also meet with Joe at a nice Chinese Restaurant for our monthly catch up on what God is doing in our lives, and oh yeah, "No. I will not marry you." He handles it great, or so I think because he always smiles after my "no." He is off to Florida, and I say, 'See you next month."

February is here. It is early, early February and cold. I go off to the ministry that has the young man who made the odd comment in January. He is one of the guys that lead worship in this group. At the end of the three usual songs, he asks to sing a new song he has written. Mr. Richard says ok. He then sings a very nice song about me. The song's name is, "Shahe." Now with a name like mine, I have to assume it is about me, right? The service finishes. He comes up and hands me a tape with the song on it and the lyrics written out and says, "God told me to sing over you." Wait, what?

I leave there that night not at peace because I leave in confusion. You see this particular ministry is special in that I had to sign papers specifically not to get involved with the participants of the Bible study outside of the facility and Bible study. It's part of volunteering there. Involvement, meaning romantically, would break major rules. I also would break my trust with Mr. Richard, he also only takes in people to this ministry who keep good boundaries. I don't want to break Mr. Richard's rules either. Part of the confusion is that God does not give you a "blessing" that breaks rules. Don't forget; God has laws, and He is the Law! Throw in that there has not been a single hint of romance, and it is a confusing situation. But, how does he know about the "God will sing over me," part? That is where I am stuck.

I also meet with Joe in February, this time at Panera. We talk about what God was doing. Joe does not mention music, write me a song, or even say the words, "God will sing over me." He just talks about God and how he has been praying and "God told me that I would marry you." Yeah, right I joke, oh did you see that (pointing out the window) a pig did NOT just fly by!" "No. I will not marry you." He handles it great, or so I think because he always smiles after my "no." He is off to Florida, and I say, 'See you next month."

I start praying for the young guy because all that is surround him is "confusion" but he was the one that said, "God told me to sing over you." I get no answers. I am asking the wrong question.

At this point, Joe has never been invited to my apartment. The farthest he can go is the apartment complex community room. I am a stickler, people! Later in the month of February, Joe comes back, and we eat supper together and I, for some reason that I can't remember, agree to go back to his house to finish talking. That was so not me. When I meet with anyone guy or girl, Joe included, I drive to the meeting place and drive myself home, ALONE! I never want to be trapped anywhere. I never intend anything to look like a date. Even this night we both drive to his house because we both drove our cars to the restaurant. I am very protective of myself. I have only ever been alone with Joe once when he picked me up, and we drove to Arabic church on a Friday night because I couldn't tell him how to get there. It's dark out in the country, people! I didn't know the street names; I just knew how to get there.

I remember sitting at the end of his couch but barely sitting on the seat itself. I was trying not to get cat hair on me for fear of making Aalia sick. My sweet girl gets very sick. I did not even take my coat off. I did not stay long. Before leaving, he walks me to the car, and it's a full moon and a gorgeous night. The stars are shining, and it's about 8:30-9 pm. It was a great conversation and for some reason I was sad. I didn't want this night to end. I leave with nothing happening that would make you think that something was about to happen. I, however, don't pray about Joe. It's no. I just know, it's a no!

It's the end of February. Man, this is a long month. Adam has started up baseball season again. I have gone to watch his game. I am an odd one. I always take my chair and sit off by myself to watch my boy play baseball. I like the shade, and I like the quiet. Yes, you can find quiet at a ball field, you just avoid the bleachers and all of the non-stop useless commentary and conversations. I have a hard time listening to people talk about such silly things as she wore this or nail color that. There are believers being persecuted in Persia for reading their Bibles and it's hard to change who I am because God has changed me so much. You are responsible for what you know and what I know is that nail color and wearing something is so not important.

I sit in my blue and yellow Joe Boxer folding chair that has a great big smiley face on it. It's an ugly chair, and I have four of them. They were a $5.00 find at Kmart over a decade ago…and not that "Kmart." The local one near the condo. I have yesterday's mail in my bag. I always carry a bag with a Bible, paper, pen, ministry newsletters, and stuff so that I can catch up on my reading. I am often in situations where I have to wait for something. No, I am not a cell phone "stare at a screen" junkie. I still have the old one. It just texts, and it allows you to make real phone calls! I ask God who I should marry, feeling in no way lead toward the young man while I pick at the letter "O" on the "Joe

Boxer" plastic letters glued onto the arm of my folding chair. I am a silly little pickle.

But today, I open up a letter from the young man that is about eight pages long. Long winded, but declaring his love and intentions for me. Again, up until this point, one comment, one song. In Rita's words, "What's up with that?" But I read it, and I close it, and I sit at the ball field, and I start praying. Why? What? How? You know the usual. I know it's a no to this relationship because God does not give you a blessing of a relationship or any other type of blessing when rules are broken. When God gives you a blessing it will be in every way, shape, and form beyond measure a real blessing. Don't forget; you will get your Ruth socks blown off! I end my prayer time with, "Lord the only reason I even keep thinking about this young man is that he somehow knows that part about You singing over me. So I ask a new question, "How does he know the part about you singing over me?"

A couple of days later, during my quiet time in my Word, God reminds me about a prayer meeting in December of 2009. It was a planned night for Bible study, but the chapel was filled up with Christmas gifts, so they moved us to a small back room. Most folks came to the chapel and saw that it was closed and went away. Only a handful found the back room prayer meeting. That night Mr. Richard went around the room and asked people to share what God was doing in their lives and what they thought He was saying about the coming year.

God revealed to me that I shared that night my secret, my gift of sweet words from the Lord that "He was going to sing over me." The young man was in the room. He heard it and decided to "make" that happen for me. The next day I ask Mr. Richard about the December meeting. I do not ask specifically because I don't want to give away my reason for asking. He confirms that he remembers me saying that and, without realizing it, during the conversation mentioned that the young man was in the room. Yup, I blew it. That's how the young man knew my "love words" from the Lord.

Let me explain. Sometimes when you are praying, the Lord will whisper to your heart or share a Bible verse that goes to your heart, and it is a special word just for you. Don't miss that, just for you. Keep those special "love words" to yourself until God lets you reveal them. Let me explain some more.

Do you remember my washer and dryer? I prayed in my head to God. My heart was heard by God and only God. I did not write it down; I did not share my need with anyone. The enemy of my soul did not hear it or read it in my journal. It was a word from me to God. Only God knows everything. Satan has to guess. He is a good guesser, a bad angel, but a good guesser. Then when God shared it with someone, I still don't know who to thank (btw thank you again and again!), it is between God and that person. The person fulfilled what God said. That person did not take credit. My family was blessed beyond measure and that blessing continued for many, many years. Nothing about the blessing was confusion (Satan), division (Satan), making me break rules (Satan), etc.

Blessings enrich and increase. Blessings encourage and uplift. Blessings show characteristics of the very character of God. Blessings last for long time periods, even from generation to generation! Blessings increase with your loved ones. Now, when you let your secret between you and God, "love words," slip out verbally or on paper, you hand Satan a weapon against you. Don't forget; even Satan will use Bible verses to trick you. How do I know, because the Bible tells me so! Don't forget about the challenges of the lusts of the eyes, lusts of the flesh, and the lust of the boastful pride of life. Satan used Scripture to try and trick Jesus Himself who then used Scripture to rebuke Satan.

Satan wants to steal, kill, and destroy. His method of operation does not change. He is a good guesser. He knows that I have been very, very careful not to let him into my world as far as dating and protecting my sexuality. I don't let myself get into alone-type of situations in meeting places or in cars. I just don't. But Satan heard my words that I shared, and he plans to use them to trick me. He wants to deceive me. He wants to trick me into a deception.

A blessing is good. It comes from God. A deception is bad. It comes from Satan. One of Satan's names is "the deceiver." The opposite of receiving a blessing is receiving a deception. I know what you are thinking, you already know that. But I do too, and yet we as believers do not apply this and respond to this spiritual truth properly.

Spiritual Truth: A deception (from Satan) always comes BEFORE a blessing (from God).

Satan wants to steal, kill, or destroy that which God intends to bless you with which includes and will affect your future in Christ Jesus. Satan wants you to fall for the deception that you perceive to be from God because you have fallen for Satan using Scripture against you or you have shared your "love words" or shared what God is doing secretly within you too early. You share it because it is exciting and you want it to happen now! But time and time again, God shares with you ALWAYS in advance of when it will happen so that you will be prepared to receive it or walk it out with Him and you will know that you are supposed to walk it out the way God intends for you to do it.

God shares it in secret to your heart because He is about changing your heart to be like His. He shares it in secret to your heart because He is in an intimate relationship with you. He shares it in secret to your heart so that no one else hears including Satan because it a secret between you.

A husband and a wife have an intimate relationship. What if one of the spouses constantly shared the intimate conversations between them with everyone around them. Then the people around them would "know" them better but that type of "knowing" is a false knowing because they only know the intimate conversations from one of the partners. It is only ever half of the story. Remember the Hebrew word, "Yada" means to intimately know and understand.

Well, Satan heard what I shared and was using the "God will sing over me part" against me by convincing the young man that he needed to "make" this happen in my life. He "made" it happen by making a song and writing a letter. The reason it was confusing is that it was not "made" by Him.

Be careful dear ones. Look out for Satan and his trickery. When I remembered why the young man knew my secret "love words," I was at peace. I had asked the right question, and I got an answer that satisfied. Always, seek peace. Peace is from God. Satan can't fake peace. If your spirit belongs to Jesus, there is only peace that transcends understanding and comes only from Jesus. Don't forget about Naomi from the Book of Ruth. Naomi was not thinking or acting like a person of faith. She made her decision on returning to the land of Judah based on what she had "heard." Never assume that the obvious is the right thing to do. Always seek to know God's will in any situation.

Satan may trick you into thinking that you are at peace, but you will know it is a false peace if you are a believer in Christ Jesus and something is "not quite right between you and God." Your deceptive blessing that you believe to be a real blessing because you have been tricked will show characteristics of its author. If God authors your blessing, you will have abundance, you will have more, you will have peace, and you will have the very characteristics of Jesus. If Satan authors your blessing, you will have less, you will have removal, you will lose things of value or virtue, and you will have the very characteristics of Satan.

Deceptive blessings lead to a lack of resources. You will be frustrated. You will be tired. You will not be able to solve something. You will take steps backward instead of forwards. You will have a season of time pass, and you will wake up and realize that you are in the same place you were at the start of that season. Or worse, you would have taken steps back, lost resources, and found yourself back where you started before the deceptive blessing came into your life. Deceptive blessings remove loved ones from your life for the wrong reasons.

Now, what if you realize that you have already accepted this deceptive blessing. Well, recognize it, realize it and repent! God will help you get out of the circumstances and consequences you are in only if you come to Him in a true spirit of repentance and reconciliation. He will not help you if you come to Him in a position of "justification." Justification is a reason, a fact, a circumstance, or explanation that justifies or defends your position.

Justification is what we do to trick ourselves into thinking that what we are currently participating in is "OK" because…. What it means is that we feel conviction from God, BUT we choose to respond to God by suppressing those feeling and doing activities and other things to numb those God-feelings. Pretty soon we don't "feel" because we are familiar with the state of "numbness." God will allow you to stay numb until you realize that you are not satisfied with numbness. You want godliness!

Looking back, I don't know why it took me so long to seek godliness. I guess I could justify my slowness by whining that the young man knew my secret "love words" from God. But I won't. I almost got tricked to accept the deception. God will never ask you to step outside of godliness to be blessed. Once this was settled in my heart, I finally looked for Jesus's blessing. It caused me to take a good look at the older guy. This man looked a whole lot like Jesus to me. Jesus is all he talked about. Jesus is all we ever talked about. I may have to stop saying never, and that pigs don't fly.

Grace and peace be multiplied to you in the knowledge of God and of Jesus our Lord; seeing that His divine power has granted to us everything pertaining to life and godliness, through the true knowledge of Him who called us by His own glory and excellence.

For by these He has granted to us His precious and magnificent promises, so that by them you may become partakers of the divine nature, having escaped the corruption that is in the world by lust. Now for this very reason also, applying all diligence, in your faith supply moral excellence, and in your moral excellence, knowledge, and in your knowledge, self-control, and in your self-control, perseverance, and in your perseverance, godliness,

And in your godliness, brotherly kindness, and in your brotherly kindness, love. For if these qualities are yours and are increasing, they render you neither useless nor unfruitful in the true knowledge of our Lord Jesus Christ.

2 Peter 1:2-8 (NASB)

Heart of Stone

March is here. I have settled the young man. No. He is the deception. I have not settled the older man. I don't want to deal with my heart. I resist change with everything in me. Why do I do that? Time and time again, God reveals my heart to me. He reveals places in my heart where I act like flesh and where I act like Him. God also reveals places where I have allowed my heart to turn to stone. A heart of stone has no place for love. Without ever realizing it, I had a heart of stone toward the Jewish people and the nation of Israel. God redeemed me and revealed to me His ways. His way is for my heart to change and repent of my attitude toward the Jewish people and the nation of Israel. Now, I love the Jewish people and the nation of Israel. I have a new heart! I have a heart like His. My heart is full of love. God is love.

Totally realizing it, meaning, because of my hurt and pain, I had a heart of stone toward Persian people and the followers of Islam. God redeemed me and revealed to me His ways. His way is for my heart to change and repent of my attitude toward Persian people and the followers of Islam. Now, I love Persian people and the followers of Islam. I have a new heart! I have a heart like His. My heart is full of love. God is love.

So, Lord, how does this apply to my stone heart and marriage? I realize that I was disobedient and that I did not marry who you chose but who I chose. You even warned me, "Don't do it." I realize that in my disobedient past, You showed me that I would have to walk out the consequences of my disobedience. You showed me to "pray for my enemy" and then changed me so that my enemy was no longer my ex-husband. You changed me to "call a nation I do not know and a nation I do not know will run to me." But seriously, marriage. I cannot handle this. I do not know how to love someone else. I love my children. How do I prepare my heart for "more?" I have no idea how to do this!

Delight yourself in the LORD; and He will give you the desires of your heart.

Psalm 37:4 (NASB)

Now I know that many people read this verse and think fluffy stories about romance, flowers, and butterflies. You think that "if you wish it, it will come." If you pray for it, it will happen. Name it and claim it. If you love it, it will come to you that which your heart desires. Stop it! Slap yourself hard enough to knock the fluff and stuff out of your thought process. Give yourself a good whack and make sure that there are no spare butterflies fluttering around in there. That is not what this verse means, people!

Delight as a verb means to please (someone) greatly. As a noun, delight means great pleasure. So take great pleasure in the Lord. Get to know and intimately understand God. You can learn more about God and who God is by reading your Bible and praying. You can also get to know more about God by listening and obeying. God reveals Himself to you through, prayer and Scripture. Praying is not a one-way wish-list, people! God also reveals Himself to you through His Names. So get to know your Husband, the Lover of Your Soul, and the God Who is Enough!

When you get to know and intimately understand more and more of God. You put more and more of Him in your heart. It's like cleaning out your old condo and getting rid of your old stuff, the stuff you don't need, and the stuff you have outgrown. When you have pushed out and cleaned out the old, you will have room for "more" in its place. This "more" is more of God. It will be "new" to you. New revelation and new illumination. Make sure dear ones that the "new" that you fill your heart up with is all about Jesus! Don't backtrack. Don't let the enemy fill up your clean spaces with muck.

Now that your heart is full of God, it brings you more delight, peace, and joy. This is a good cycle to be in. The more you do this, the more of God you let in your heart and the less room you have for fluffy stuff and stuff that is not of God.

When God changes your heart, He makes it new. But the "new" is not "all about you, people!" This "new" means Him. He changes your heart to be like His heart. Don't miss that! Your heart changed by God becomes more like God's heart.

When the verse goes on to say and "He will give you the desires of your heart," that does not mean you get the great paying job, perfect family, and no worries. That means your changed heart looks like His heart and God will give you the desires of your heart which look like His heart! Confused?

When your heart changes to be more like His, your "desires" which are, petitions and requests change to be more like His too. Instead of wanting selfish petitions and requests, you start thinking selflessly. You start to change, and you want what God wants. When you want what God wants, then you are once again aligning with the Will of God. God answers the prayers that fulfill His purposes and His plans.

Now back to my stone heart. I have to recognize that part of my heart that I say can "Never" be healed. I have to realize that I have a bad attitude. I have to realize that I have been disobedient. I have to realize that I have been unprepared. I have to realize that I have been unfruitful. I have reached a place in my walk with my Lord that I have a choice to make.

My past is Moab. I have completed that part. I have left that place, and I am on a journey to a new place. This place is a provision of life. I have a choice to make. I can choose to be like Orpah and be stiff-necked, stubborn, and return to my old ways. I can go back and live in Moab. Although, I'm pretty sure that Moabites are Persians in disguise!

My future is Bethlehem. Bethlehem means house of bread. I can choose to be like Ruth and be obedient, yielding, with a serving heart. I need to be ready to repent and respond when someone in "position" says, "be prepared and get thee to the threshing floor."

So how do I get prepared? For me, I start to "remember" what God has already done in my life.

For me to move forward, I have to know my history and there is nothing wrong with being honest with God. I have, to be honest and recognize where I have not yielded or where I have not been obedient. My "desires" of my heart have changed. I no longer "desire" my old ways. I want God's ways. I want God to say, "That's my girl!"

God told me long ago, "Don't hang onto the stone, it will make you drown." I let go! I even threw some of those stones across the Jordan River! I let go because of Jesus!

God showed me that my heart was capable of being in a season of drought. It was capable of being so dry that the Living Water would roll off of the dryness and remove the good soil. So I read my Word and bathed my heart with the Living Water to keep my heart soft and usable. I am usable because of Jesus!

God showed me that wedges, cracks, and division are the enemy. My heart would never be whole unless I let Jesus heal the places that I had let wedges, cracks, and division grow. I prayed for healing and let Jesus bind, heal, and close up the space between the divides. I am healed because of Jesus!

God showed me that I could live and survive places that I thought that I could not, or would not, live in, like *that city*. So He sent me there, and I returned. I overcame because of Jesus!

God showed me that doors may have closed in areas of my life but that He is The Door. He has also shown me that "open windows" can be a blessing. I am thankful that I can roll down my window and play in the wind when the circumstances in life turn up the heat. I have open doors and open windows because of Jesus!

God showed me that even the things that seem small like travel-size tide could be big if I purpose myself to complete what God calls important. I make the tasks of my day about Him. I have prioritized my life to make God the priority because of Jesus!

I can go on and on so I put one foot forward. I try not to look back to "Moab" but to "remember" what God has done. It changes me from being defined by this world's definitions to being defined by God's definition. I am an overcomer because of Jesus.

Joe calls one morning and asks a favor. He has had a kidney stone, and he drove himself to the hospital. The hospital he drove himself to transferred him by ambulance to another larger hospital. He has just returned home and needs a ride to go and get his car from the hospital parking lot. I get off the phone and Aalia and I decide to help. We make him give us the keys to his car and stay home. We head off to find a car that I can barely remember how it looks. Aalia is brilliant. She suggests popping the trunk, and we instantly find it. We drive it back to his house. The next day I take food over, and his sister has just arrived to help take of him. Joe doesn't look good. I really like his sister. For the next several days, I make excuses after work to go check in on Joe, but I really am going to see Paula. I am honest and tell Joe that.

Monday morning rolls around and I have to fix food to feed the eleven o'clock Bible study. I head to the store. A friend asks if I can keep her middle schooler for the day. I said yes if she can run around with me. My co-volunteer Ms. Carol doesn't have a car today, and she calls to see if I can pick her up on the way. In the meantime, I have agreed to drop Joe off at the doctor's to get his kidney stint removed. I don't even know what that means, but I drop him off at the hospital, take Ms. Carol and Cassie to the apartment complex. We serve lunch and have Bible study. We then pick up this poor white as a ghost white man from the hospital. Joe doesn't look good. I take Ms. Carol home and then Cassie. Poor Joe just sits there in silence. I drop him home, and we don't talk much. I think he just wants to go in his house and die. I run supper over later, but he is sick. I think I've killed him.

The following Tuesday Joe comes to Bible study. He is looking much better. Mr. Richard walks in with food. The store did not have individual servings of chicken, so he has brought three cooked whole chickens and all of the fixings. He tells me to wash my hands and pull it apart so that we can serve it. Wait, what? Touch chicken…meat…bare hands…no gloves? I have issues, people!

I don't do well with meat and bones and especially dismantling it. I struggle to be obedient. It's not a clean environment. No knives, just plastic forks, and plates. Ugh! Seeing my fear, Joe steps in. He washes his hands and gets to work. He pulls three chickens apart and puts the meat on plates so that the guests could just pick up a plate and move on to get the fixings.

Why is this man so nice? I just stare. I work quietly beside him until everyone has food. As we start to clean up, I head to the room next door to find paper towels. I come back, and there is Joe, standing in the center of the room, looking right at me with a grin on his face and joy in his eyes and he just out and says, "I love you." Wait, what?

Love? You love me. I even ask him, "How can you say that?" He just says, "I just know that I do. God has given me a love for you." Now, we are standing in a room full of people who seem to be frozen in time or oblivious to the man in the middle with two hands covered in chicken flesh. Gross. This is not the romantic moment I thought could come my way. But his face. He has joy. Well, I honestly do not. I am not there yet. I have issues, people!

I drive away fussing at God. How can he just say that? "I love you" are just words that people say and the words don't mean anything. People just say it because it's easy or sounds good. "Bye, love you." I don't trust I love you's! In my frustration, I turn on the radio. A song comes on, and the first line that I hear is, "You say love is just a word, four letters in a row…" Ok, this song has my attention. I think yeah, see, people just use that word too much. The song goes on, and it is matching up with my attitude. But then the words change, "there is a way, there is a spark, hope you can hold on to, there is a lifeline come to rescue you…" You need to go hear this song, "There Is A Way" by NewWorldson. Oh my, I am a tearful basket case. The words are piercing me. Even the words "lifeline" which is the ministry I work for and "flesh" which is Joe standing there having served for me and done something that I did not want to do. He is right there. This song uses one of my most favorite verses, John 14:6. I am undone.

I move over in traffic to take the exit and before my turn, I sit at a red light. I am still in tears, and I see the license place in front of me, "IMLOVED." That's it. I am undone, all over again. I go home and for a couple of days, try to comprehend all of this.

It is now the end of March and my one year lease on the apartment is coming up for renewal. I receive a letter stating that my rent is going down by almost a hundred dollars! Yeah, thank you, God! I go off to sign up at the office. The office lady takes one look at the letter and says that there is a mistake, my rent is going up almost a hundred dollars. She wants to keep my letter and show her boss. I stick up for myself and tell her that she can make a copy but that I will keep the letter and come back tomorrow.

I return the next day to find out that they have to honor my letter. I am going to get almost a hundred dollars off of my monthly rent. I am so proud for standing up for myself. I am a chicken at heart. So I start to sign the lease, and I have all different time frames which to choose. Six months is the smallest and three years is the longest. I pray that I make the right choice. I finished reading the lease and returned to the place where I selected the time frame. I choose six months. Wait, what? This time, I didn't say this! The property manager did. She cannot believe that I chose the smallest time frame. Before she signs it, she even warns me that next time the lease will be for the new full price and not the mistake price. I tell her that I don't understand it either because I have no plans to move, but God would not let my hand go to the other options. I'm sure she is thinking, "This girl is too mystical."

I walk home so excited that I stuck up for myself and that I am going to save money. Joe calls on my way up; he wants to let me know that he is going to the food and clothing ministry in the morning. I tell him my good news, and he sounds upset. He even kind of sounds mad but not mean mad, just unexpected and kind of sad mad. He sounds frustrated. Now, I am mad. I am so excited and feel like a financial genius, and he is frustrated? It's a short call. I stomp up the many stairs to my third-floor apartment and declare to the Lord that I am never talking to Joe Nahler again!" Who does he think he is anyway! He should be happy for me! Door slam and all.

The next morning I get up, my mother is still at my brother's house helping with the baby. We have her car, and I send the kids off to school. I get in the truck to head up to the food and clothing ministry. I pull up to the main apartment complex gate. My truck dies right in front of the gate. Ugh! I am going to be late! I do a dance to try and trigger the gate open. Finally, a man comes along, and he triggers the gate so that I can push my truck down the hill and park it out of the way. Yes, you read it right. He watched me push the truck. Thanks, buddy! I don't know what to do. It is an early morning, but everyone around me would already be at work...except Joe.

Seriously, I told you, God! I don't want to talk to him ever again! But I look through my contact list, and I can't find anyone available. UGH! I call Joe. He agrees to come and get me, and we go off to the food and clothing ministry. It's getting late, and there is no time to deal with the truck. After we finish, we come back to the truck. He looks it over, and it needs to be towed to the shop. Ugh!

A couple of days pass and my truck is ready. I get a call from the shop, it' was just a fuel filter. Easy fix. I pick it up and resume my ways. I thank God for my truck. I am still not there yet for Joe.

Looking back, well, I have to admit that I sure am a stubborn half-ghani. That's my new term for half-American and half-Afghani. Half-ghani! I like it. I also have to admit that even as a believer I can still be fleshy, even chicken fleshy. I am not perfect. I will never be perfect in this lifetime while I wear this flesh suit. I have Jesus. He is in the process of making me perfect, but I will not be perfect until I get my eternity suit! I hope, I am taller! Five feet would be nice!

I find out later that Joe consulted God daily about marrying me and that every time I turned him down, even though he smiled, it made him very sad. I even made him cry once.

I find out much later that Joe consulted with the car shop. It seems that it was a fuel pump that needed to be replaced and not just the fuel filter. He paid for a lot more to be repaired on my truck than I ever realized at the time. He never said a word to me. Not one. I did not find this out until after we were married.

I also find out much, much later that Joe consulted with Mr. Richard. He talked to Mr. Richard sometime back in 2009; he can't remember exactly. What he does remember is that he asked Mr. Richard if he was too old to date me. Evidently, there was some dancing on Mr. Richard's part and something about saying,

"This is too much, this is just too much!" After ten minutes, he finally settled down from his silliness and said, "She will be fine with it, but you will have to be patient, really patient." He rebounded back into silly land. This does not surprise me. Mr. Richard likes silly land.

The LORD your God is with you, he is mighty to save. He will take great delight in you, he will quiet you with his love, he will rejoice over you with singing.

Zephaniah 3:17 (NIV)

I Have A Heart

April is here. I have yet to settle the older man. I am trying, people! About mid-April Joe and I spend a weekend together. No, not like that. We ate dinner on Friday night. We had the whole day Saturday and Sunday together. He is about to go back to Florida to spend time with family. This time, our conversations are different. It's still about God, but we get to know each other a lot better.

This time, we talk about our kids. Joe has a daughter and a son. His daughter is married and has two kids, and they live in Florida. He has a son who is also married, and they live in France. He has met my kids, but I have been very protective of them. I don't let anyone close to my kids if there is any way possible that they can get hurt.

It is a nice weekend, and I finally let my wall come down. Joe is very funny. He is very smart too, but I think that the most attractive part of him is that he loves Jesus. I tell him that I don't need a rescuer, that I already have one. But before I can say I want someone who will make me number two because God is number one, he says, "Well, you will never be first in my life, God is." Ugh!

I tell him that there is just no way that God would bring us together because you have three cats, and Aalia cannot be around cats at all. He tells me that he has already prayed about it, and he knows homes that the cats can go. Ugh!

I tell him that there is just no way that God would bring us together because he drinks alcohol and I do not want ever to be around an alcoholic husband again. He tells me that he will quit drinking. He's prayed about it, and he will just stop drinking. Ugh!

It doesn't matter what I throw at him; he answers that he has prayed about it. Ugh!

The weekend ends, and he leaves on Tuesday. I promise to pray about marrying him. I have yet to do that. So far I have…fussed, whined, argued, stomped my feet, and even slammed a door. I guess it's time to pray!

I call him Monday night before he leaves, I ask to come over. He is about seven minutes away. I want to talk for just a minute, and then I will go back home. I had been praying about moving specifically to his home. I thought it might be awkward to live in the home that he had lived in with his wife that died of cancer. They had lived in this home for about eight years. They had been married for over 36 years when she died. The home did not "feel" like me, and I wasn't sure I could do it. I had been praying about the home, and God got me settled down. "You will be fine; the home is fine. He will let you make changes so that you will feel comfortable."

My whole purpose was to go over to the actual home after God said, "You will be fine, the home is fine. He will let you make changes so that you will feel comfortable." But I sat on the end of the couch much the same way as that other time and yup; I still felt uncomfortable. I am just about to tell him how uncomfortable, and he says, "Shahe, I've been praying about it, and we can make any changes around the house that you would like to make so that you feel more comfortable." Ugh!

I've got nothing, people! I HAVE to start praying about this guy. I don't want to, but I have lost my defenses. He goes off to Florida. I start to pray. Oh, yeah, I leave for Italy and Greece with Aalia in June, and I am going to leave the school group and connect with the Bible study group in Istanbul. We are traveling through Turkey and Greece and studying the churches of Revelation and Paul's journey. A group of six ladies from our church is studying Paul's journey on Wednesday nights.

I call my friend, and this is the first Wednesday during this whole time of the study group that I have had time to meet her for dinner before going to the Bible study. We start to eat, and we are talking. I am finally getting the nerve up to say something about Joe. I start with telling her about different aspects about Joe. Every time I say something like, "He is nice and…." She counters with, "Well that will change after you are married." Then she would go on to tell about her recent remarriage. One by one I would throw up a comment and get back "that will change." I am getting seriously freaked out, people! I never thought about any of this stuff. I am panicking.

She goes off to get a drink refill, and I sit there panicking! What if Joe changes when we are married, and I can't get a divorce and be divorced twice, and I let my head start a marathon down an ugly racetrack? She sits back down, and I ask her for the first time about her new husband, "Why is your husband, not married to his wife that he had the kids with?" She proceeds to tell me that they are divorced and that she is his third wife, he was married for a short time in between her and the mother of his kids. Oh, so I reason and try to calm my poor heart down. She is her husband's third wife. Maybe that's why stuff changed after getting married. I kept thinking, "Whew, I am just Joe's second. His wife died of cancer. He did not divorce her."

We go off to Bible study and the study which has been all about Paul's missionary journey suddenly gets off into the Fruit of the Spirit. Specifically, going down the list, I sat and listened and looked down and saw this list. I saw where Joe was mature in the Fruit of the Spirit, and I was lacking. He and his life showed great maturity in love, joy, peace, patience (he had to have that, or he wouldn't survive me), kindness, goodness, gentleness, faithfulness, and self-control. God showed me where I lacked in that very same list. I came away that night shaken by my friend and steadied by my Faithful Father God.

So I earnestly prayed about marrying Joe. Yes, I finally prayed about and used the words, "marrying Joe." Ugh! I pray that the Lord show me a sign and if I missed the sign that I should marry Joe that God would slap me and make sure that I "see" it because I don't want to miss what God is doing."

May is here. I have decided to settle the older man. I really am trying, people! For the next few days from Thursday until Saturday I pray for the Lord to show me a sign.

In the meantime, both of my children are in their school play. So the weekend is very, very busy. I rush here and help them with this and that. I watch the performance twice, and I am planning to see it one more time on Saturday night. With all of the rushing around with the kids, I keep praying about marrying Joe. *Lord, please show me a sign!* I also, keep finding dimes everywhere. I never find money. This is new to me. I even walk into the church office one day, and as I am disarming the alarm, Cathy comes up behind me and say, "Here's your dime. You dropped a dime." That's not my dime?

Aalia also has her prom on Friday night. It has been a very busy week. I can sum it up with three simple words; kids, praying and dimes. The kids were easy. Aalia's a senior and her senior year is winding down. I cannot believe my beautiful baby girl is growing up so fast. My joy filled son is too, but he has two more years of school. The praying is easy to do, but God is easy to pray to. I love having a God that I can pray to and He hears me and answers. And well, then there are those dimes. I have no clue, people!

It has been raining for days. Saturday morning it starts to get scary. They start issuing flash flood warnings. By early afternoon, I decide to drive over the highway bridge and get to the kids. They are already at school to get ready for the play tonight. Just as I cross over the bridge, Aalia calls and they are going to cancel the play; there is too much water at the school. I arrive, and the parking lot is filling up fast. I am so thankful to get the kids home before the flooding gets worse. Worse turns into flooding everywhere. Record-breaking rainfall and a once in a lifetime flood. Thank you, Jesus, for a third-floor apartment building!

I call Joe later with the intention of telling him, "Yes, I will marry you." There is a part of me wondering if the one in a hundred year flood is the sign from God. As we talk, I make a comment before I say yes. I casually tell him that I keep finding "money" everywhere and before I can say, "what does that mean." He says, "I know; I keep finding dimes everywhere. I never find money." Well, that's it. It was the dime. During our conversation, I did finally say yes. We did both throws around the word "dime" and wondered what it meant. It was not until we stopped calling it a "dime" and starting thinking the number "ten" that we finally got a clue.

Ten is the number of completion. Ten is a very good number.

I ended the called with, "So when do you want to do this?" He replied, "I get back tomorrow so how about tomorrow?" I would whack him, but he is in Florida. "No, seriously, when do you want to get married?" He asks when my lease is up, so I go and look. I come back and tell him, October 9th is when my lease ends. He laughs and says, "How about October 10th, it's a Sunday. We can get married on 10-10-2010, at 2:10 pm."

Looking back, I can't help but quote the Tin Man from the Wizard of Oz. "I have a heart!" Or I guess to make it sound more like me, "I have a heart, people! Who knew?" Pigs fly! They can you know! Who knew?

Well, Joe did not get back the next day which is a Sunday. The flooding continued to flood our whole area, and it was really bad. Even the airport got closed for a day, and he could not get a flight in until Monday. Good thing we decided to wait until October to get married. I gotta go sit down, people! This is too much, this is just too much!

I will sing a new song to You, O God; upon a harp of ten strings, I will sing praises to You.

Psalm 144:9 (NASB)

Still May

It is still May. I have settled the older man. I am getting married, people! Our metro area and surrounding counties are devastated by flood waters. Things that were once familiar are gone and will have to be rebuilt. Our area is changing. My "familiar" has also been washed away, and I don't plan to rebuild those walls. My life is changing fast.

I can remember holding the most beautiful baby girl in my arms after a very hard delivery and thinking that she was the most beautiful baby I had ever seen. Ok, yes, I did say that she looked like a pink monkey, but I was on drugs, people! After the drugs had worn off, I said she was beautiful. She was so tiny and little in every way. Nothing chubby, not even her cheeks. That is when I started saying, "she has cute chubby toes." My baby girl is graduating high school! God's promise has come about in that my daughter is graduating from her private Christian school. Only God could have accomplished this! To Him be the glory!

Since my dad is not around, and my mother is up at my brother's house. I tell Joe that he needs to do the Persian "thing" and ask my kids if he can marry me. I explain that it involves bringing fruit and candy. Persians dress up the plate pretty and put fabric and bows around the dishes. I explain that it involves bringing flowers and jewelry. Persians love flowers, but jewelry seals the deal. We set up a time for him to talk with the kids.

The kids and I set up a time to give him the other parts of the test that I left out. Persians will ask lots of questions and "tests" of worthiness. The kids and I decide that they will come up with 100 questions (10x10) to ask him and only if he answers them to their satisfaction will he pass the test. We also come up with four skills tests.

Joe arrives with a dish that he has lovingly prepared with candy and fresh fruit and lots of pretty flowers. The kids welcome him in and start in on him with the questions.

Test #1 Candy Bars

They show him four full-size candy bars and tell him to assign a family member to each type of candy. This is a test to see how well he knows each of us. One is peanut butter cups (Adam), one is cookies and cream (Aalia), one is coconut (mommy), and the other is dark chocolate (Joe). He figures it out and passes the test.

Test #2 Read This

They joke it is an intelligence test. They hand him piece of paper and ask him to read this:

MR DUCKS
MR NOT
MR TOO
CDMEDBD FEETS
LIB
MR DUCKS

Test #3 Endurance Test

Aalia and I did not let Adam in on this one. We put a shallow baking sheet pan on the kitchen island. We filled it with water. Joe and Adam are on each end of the pan. Keeping their hands on the island their task is to blow a toothpick to the other side of the pan. The first one to get the toothpick to the other side wins. I have the camera to record it. Aalia stands in the middle; they lower their heads to prepare to blow the toothpick. Aalia says, "Ready, set, go!" She then slaps the pan, and they both get wet. Joe is laughing so hard that he turns a very red color. He has a white beard, so the kids think that he is too funny.

Test # 4 Humor Test

To be in our family, you will need humor. It's a coping mechanism, people! The kids decide to show him a video that involves a ventriloquist that has a dummy named, "The Dead Terrorist." They figure that if he doesn't laugh, he is going to be in real trouble. I think this video hits a cord with the kids and me because it makes light of a very real thing that we three deal with everyday. We get judged a lot and "profiled" by how we look. That is where the humor comes in. You just deal with it and hopefully with humor.

Some of the 100 Questions (His Answers)

1. Can we have a dog? (Joe said yes, I said no)
2. How many animals did Moses put on the ark? (Zero, Moses wasn't on the ark)
3. What's mom's favorite color? (None, she loves to paint and loves all of the colors)
4. If Adam begs for a caffeinated Coke, will you let him? (No!)
5. If we went out to eat, which place would we go, Chick fil A, KFC, or Papa John's? (Chick fil A, because of dairy allergy)
6. How many times a day does Mr. Richard call mom? (Way too many)
7. Will you sit there and let me shoot paintballs at you? (No, but Adam was hoping for a yes)
8. Do you like Dean Martin music? (Yes)
9. Do you shred papers or throw them away? (My kids know my pet peeves!)
10. Are you prepared for long lines and long waits in airports when mom gets pulled over? (They know me so well!)

This was just a sample. I figured ten was good enough. As you can see, my kids are funny. They are sick and wrong like their mama. He gives me a lovely engagement ring. And he fits right into our little family. You need to pray seriously for Joe! Aalia graduates high school, and we prepare for our trip to Italy and Greece.

We also had one other funny moment. Adam's baseball season was greatly delayed because of the flood waters. Most of the area ball fields were underwater or damaged. At his game last night, Joe and I are sitting in my famous smiling Joe Boxer chairs. Joe tells me that he has something that he has wanted to share with me for a while now, but he hopes this is not a game changer. Ok, I'm ready. I have no idea what he is about to say. He goes on to explain that he was married before. Yup, I knew that. No, he means, before the marriage of over 36 years. He was married for about nine months back when he was in the Navy. It didn't work out, and he got divorced. Wait, what?

Will I be your third wife? I do not react the way he thought I would. I break out laughing and almost fall out of my smiling chair. The first thing that comes to mind is the night that my friend kept saying, "That will change after marriage." And I remember consoling myself by saying that I would be Joe's second wife. Ha! I am in tears. I am also relieved. I had been very intimidated to marry such a wonderful man that was married for 36 years, and I could only last six years in my first marriage! So we are both divorced for the same reason. No, it is not a deal breaker, but it is extremely funny. I know he is very relieved to have it all finally out there. I can't imagine the pressure he had been feeling. I am glad he told me, but I tell him, nice try, you are stuck with me now!

Looking back, it was just perfect, and Joe is not even Persian! He did great. God reminded me of the little lady who prayed for me back in Israel. She prayed for me to have a husband and handed me five red strings. I have kept those red strings without ever knowing what they meant. Well, this is May 10th, five years later from that first trip to Israel. Maybe the red strings meant years to wait. Maybe five was "incomplete" and she prayed for me to be complete. Either way, it is a sweet thought to think.

We still laugh at all of this. I wish I could show you the video. I have always watched the kids diets so much so that they won't get caffeine and or too much sugar. Joe had brought them a lovely tray full of fresh fruit and candy. They kept stuffing their mouths full and asking him questions. Of course, Aalia ate all of the fruit and Adam ate the gummy worms and bears. I guess some things never change!

One other thought about never say never.

You remember me talking about what is in your heart needs to be what is in God's heart? Psalm 37:4, people! Well, the Bible also talks about what comes out of your mouth is what is in your heart. This also means what is in your heart comes out of your mouth. If your mouth says, "never" then your heart says, "never."

195

God can change your heart if you let Him. God changes your heart to make your heart be more like His heart. The more your heart is like His heart, the more you are in one accord with the Lord. Then what comes out of your mouth will be in accord with what is in your heart. What is in your heart will be in one accord with the Lord.

Warning! Never say never, because God will use Luke 1:37 on you!

Here are a few examples from my personal "never" list:

- *I said I was never going to that city. Yup, been there.*
- *I said I would never go to "Target." Yup, been there.*
- *I said I would never become a Christin. Yup, I am one.*
- *I said I would never witness to Jews or Muslims. Yup, I do that.*
- *I said I would never have more kids after Aalia. Yup, hello Adam.*
- *I said I would never get divorced. Yup, I did that.*
- *I said I would never remarry...O Lord! Yes, I did say that. And yes, I will!*

Here are a few examples off of God's personal "never" list:

- *God told Abraham he would be a father and Sarah would be the mother of Isaac.*
- *Saul of Tarsus who persecuted the followers of Jesus became Paul the Apostle of Jesus.*
- *Peter said he would never deny Jesus, but he did three times.*
- *Joseph said he would never forgive his brothers for what they did to him, but he did.*
- *Pharaoh said he would never let the Hebrews go free, but he did.*
- *Jonah said that he would never go to Nineveh, but he did.*
- *People told Noah, it is never going to rain.*

I think that the greatest "never" that a person can have that can damage their eternal future is to say that they "never" need a

Lord and a Savior. That, my dear ones, breaks my heart. I know that it breaks God's heart too.

For He Himself has said, "I will never desert you, nor will I ever forsake you," so that we confidently say, "The LORD is my helper, I will not be afraid. What will man do to me?" Remember those who led you, who spoke the word of God to you; and considering the result of their conduct, imitate their faith. Jesus Christ is the same yesterday and today and forever.

Hebrews 13:5-8 (NASB)

But what comes out of the mouth proceeds from the heart, and this defiles a person. For out of the heart come evil thoughts, murder, adultery, sexual immorality, theft, false witness, slander.

Matthew 15:18-19 (ESV)

June

I start off thinking the month of June will be a traveling month and that July-September will be preparation to be married months. What I will discover later is that it will take all four months to get me ready for marriage.

Aalia and I and her school group head off to Greece and then to Italy. We land in Greece and tour Athens. We go to see the Acropolis and climb to the top to see the Parthenon. While at the top of the mountain, I keep asking where Mars Hill was. This is a school trip and not a Bible study trip. Someone pointed to a bare rock spot across the valley. I take a picture, but I cannot shake the feeling that I had missed something. We visit lots of places in Greece including Delphi.

From Greece, we take a boat to Italy. In Italy, we go to Rome and tour the many places that most tourists visit. I enjoy time with my daughter and her sweet friend Holly, but there is a part of me that is sad that this tour is not more than just a tour. We are missing the opportunity as a group of believers to tour with "Biblical eyes." Sure we shop and see famous fountains, but we walk right past churches and places that could deepen the walk for the young adults who are with us. Never miss an opportunity to pour into young people. Teach them Biblical history so that it comes alive for them. I know it is easier to do the worldly tour, but the worldly tour will leave you feeling shallow and unfulfilled.

We also visit Florence, Sorrento, Capri, and Pompeii. I like Vatican City. It is very small. The square that I have seen many times on television looked very big but in real life, it seems very small. I walk the hallways full of artistic masterpiece after masterpiece. It is too much. There is so much to see that I did not get to experience any of it in a personal way. It is summer and busy, and the crowds are huge. We get shuffled along, and we miss a lot of what I had been hoping to see.

It made me think of life. How often are we anticipating or expect something that when it finally comes about we find ourselves disappointed because we do not have the time to invest and experience it intimately so that it becomes a part of us. I have walked and spent lots of time in many different types of houses of worship. Some have mud domes, and some have galleries full of the greatest artworks of mankind. Neither one will be equal to the intimacy that you will have with the God of the Universe when you make your heart a place for Him to be welcomed into.

My daughter and her classmates board a plane in Rome to go home. I board a plane from Rome to go to Istanbul, Turkey to meet up with the Biblical study group. Some of my most favorite people are here including Dr. Bob and Rita, Hal and Shirley, Robin and Dr. Pat, along with our study ladies Rita, Kris, Carol, Elaine, and Lori.

We visit Hagia Sophia which means "Devine Wisdom" museum. It was built as a church only to be destroyed by an earthquake and rebuilt again to be destroyed by fire. The building that we see today was taken over by the Muslims and made into a mosque. My favorite part is listening to the guide talk about how the Muslims "covered up" and destroyed the markings on the building that identified it as a church. They plastered over the large face of Christ in one of the main areas only for the plaster to fall and reveal Christ's face behind the black plaster. I see it this way, the building itself is just a building. It can be destroyed by earthquakes, fire, and rebuilt. Muslims can try to cover up and deny the divinity of Christ, but even in darkened places and black plastered over hearts, He will be revealed! God will reveal Himself to each and every person He has ever created, and we choose to plaster over His face or close off our hearts.

Another funny moment came in the Basilica Cistern. It is an amazing underground water structure that provided clean water for a whole city, but my favorite part is that in building it they needed more stone bases, so they used an old head of the pagan Medusa to support the column. The head is turned sideways and is underwater. Seems fitting. This was done because the people that built the cistern did not believe in the god that the people who made the Medusa head did. To me, I see that one man's god that is lifted up is not the same god that another man lifts up. What one man will worship or fear, another man will make use of to hold up a column. That is not who Christ is. He is the real deal, people!

We visit the Topkapi Palace which was the home of an Ottoman king. This place was built to show the greatness of the man and a fountain built to provide the people with water. The sultan built it "so that they would praise him." No kingdom or empire of man will ever last and the Living Water that Christ alone supplies, is the only one that will satisfy your thirst.

I find a four-leaf clover there while waiting in line to see the palace's jewelry display. The guide tells me that I was lucky. I told him that there is no such thing as luck. He says, "Good luck is how you found the four-leaf clover." I tell him, "No way, I just asked God for the four leaf clover." Wait, what? I go on to explain that my friend Rita is always finding four-leaf clovers, and she just reached over in this small patch of greenery and found one. I then made a little prayer to God, "I never find four-leaf clovers, and I wish I could find one just for fun." And I looked up and there it was. He says, "So God is giving you good luck!" UGH! No, God is answering a prayer. I just wanted to find one to find one. I don't believe in luck. God and I have a relationship, and this is one of the ways that He is showing me that He is listening to my prayers, even the little ones that are just fun." Pray for this man. He didn't get it.

Grand Bazaars and Spice Markets and a boat ride on the Bosphorus waterway fills our days. We drink apple tea as we pass palace after palace. Some are ancient Baroque palaces, and some are modern Russian Mafia built. Either way, I will take my palace in eternity, thank you! Istanbul is a place of transition. It is both in Europe and Asia. It has many different faiths and many different trades and markets come to buy and sell in this place. It will play a major part in the transition at the end of days as the world focuses on Jerusalem.

My birthday gets celebrated in Troy; it is the ancient city that everyone remembers because of the Greek's use of the wooden horse as a gift of peace to deceive the people of Troy. Be careful dear ones that the gift of peace that you accept is only from the Prince of Peace. All others will be a deception. That which you celebrate and lift up if it is not of God will bring you down a sinful path and sin is death! We've talked about this, people! We stay the night in Canakkale. It is a lovely place and some in our group are going to participate in a Turkish Bath. Not me!

Lots of the ladies signed up. I even ask the hotel staff who is signing up the ladies what the Turkish Bath is. It's like a steam bath. I have had bad spa experiences, people! I made sure that I could leave my bathing suit on. I even ask if Rita and I can sign up together to go at the same time. "Sure, sure, no problem" is the liar's reply.

We go up to the room and change. It's my turn, and I go down to the spa. Where's Rita? I ask and the lady down there says, "No, just one." Oh well, a man comes out and tells me to go into the sauna for five minutes. I do, but it's not comfortable. There is a really large man in there who just stares at me. I am so not relaxed. I love towels, and my bathing suit, and I keep thanking God for no sign of mud or plastic wrap.

A young man comes in and tells me to follow him. So I do, and we come to a lovely blue and white tiled room with a small dome in the middle. There are little niches all the way around the room with a center island of mosaic tiles. The room is hot and steamy. The young man brings a scrubby-like hand mitt and tries to bath me. Wait, what? No way! He tries to explain as we wrestle the mitt. If I need scrubbed, I will do it thank you. He then tells me to lie down for a massage. I agree but insist on a towel over my bathing suit.

I start to think that I am a lunatic for even trying this again and plan on ways to kill Rita for talking me into this. He then tells me to roll over and take down my bathing suit top so he can continue to massage me. Yup, time to go! I get up with a "no way", and he says that he is not done. I tell him that he is, and he says that he needs to wash my hair. No, thanks and I bid him farewell. The whole time the large sauna man has been sitting in a niche. I guess he will be next, but I am gone! This is so not relaxing, people!

I later find out that Rita's name was added to the list, but it was added to the next lady's name on the list. It so figures. But the day ended well. I get an unexpected call from Joe to wish me a happy birthday. I don't know how in the world he has found me in the middle of Turkey, but he did, and I am very grateful. I also miss him and the kids terribly. I have been away about sixteen days. I have to confess that I have been unfaithful in a Turkish Spa with a younger man and he laughs at me. I also have to confess that I realize that my heart is changing. I really miss him and wish that he was here.

We visited Alexandria Troas, Smyrna, Pergamum (Bergama). Pergamum is the third church of the seven churches listed in the Book of Revelation. Messiah is revealed here as "The One who has the sharp two-edged sword." The Bible refers to the Word of God as a two-edged sword, and this is the place that parchment was invented, and parchment put together can make a book. The Word of God can divide and judge.

For the word of God is living and active and sharper than any two-edged sword, and piercing as far as the division of soul and spirit, of both joints and marrow, and able to judge the thoughts and intentions of the heart.

Hebrews 4:12 (NASB)

Smyrna is the second of the seven churches listed in the Book of Revelation. Messiah is revealed here as "The first and the last, who was dead and has come to life." This place is named for the myrrh trees that grow here; Myrrh was given to Christ when he was in Bethlehem as a young child as part of the three named gifts from the Magi. Myrrh is used in treating bodies for burial.

The next day we visit Thyatira, Sardis, and Philadelphia. Thyatira is the fourth church of the seven churches listed in the Book of Revelation. Messiah is revealed here as "The Son of God, who has eyes like a flame of fire, and His feet are like burnished bronze." It is the place of Lydia, the seller of purple dyed fabric. I find it interesting that the Messiah is revealed as "The Son of God" with all authority in a place that sells items made of purple, the color that represents man's royalty. Christ is both Son of Man and

Son of God. His eyes like a flame of fire represent understanding with judgment (fire), and His feet of bronze means strength. The deep thoughts of Satan include wanting mankind to worship himself instead of God. To worship God is to acknowledge His authority in our lives. Be careful not to be seduced away from the ways of God.

Sardis is the fifth of the seven churches listed in the Book of Revelation. Messiah is revealed as "He who has the seven Spirits of God and the seven stars." Sardis means "Prince of Joy." This is the place of the Church that has fallen asleep but is alive and is told to "wake up!" I can't help but think about how many of us walk around in our daily lives as if we are numb or asleep to the things of God. We need to "Wake up!" We need to be about the things of God, people! That is the only way to have joy in our lives. Joy is not an emotion like "happiness." Joy is a fruit of the spirit and a gift from God!

Philadelphia is the sixth of the seven churches listed in the Book of Revelation. Messiah is revealed here as "He who is holy, who is true, who has the key of David, who opens and no one will shut, and who shuts and no one opens." Messiah is shown here to have three major attributes holy (sinless), true (cannot lie), and key (power). When you stand in this place called the church of Philadelphia, all that remains are three very large columns that have stood firm when all else has fallen around them. Think of these columns as the three attributes of Christ's character. Because if we have Christ (His holiness, His truth, His power) we can walk in faith and obedience in our daily lives.

The next day we visit Colossae which is an unexcavated mound of dirt, and we drive on to Laodicea. Laodicea is the seventh of the seven churches listed in the Book of Revelation. Messiah is revealed here as "The Amen, the faithful and true Witness, the Beginning of the creation of God." Laodicea is in a valley and was a very rich community of people. The sheep would drink the water from springs that were enriched with minerals, and their wool would naturally turn black. This wool was very valuable thus making this place wealthy and self-sufficient. Laodicea was accused of being lukewarm neither hot nor cold. It is located in a valley was between a mountain of white cliffs from the minerals that resembled snow and a mountain that was barren and very hot. The people of Laodicea were not passionate for God, but they were not cold either. They were lukewarm, self-sufficient, and not dependent on God. They thought that they had all that they needed in their daily lives.

Our guide shows us a recent find of a menorah with a cross arising from the servant candle and flanked by the strong arm and an olive branch on either side. For all of the "wealth" of this community which was famous for the black wool, there was little left of "worth." Christ can leave a mark on our lives in a way that when we are gone, His mark remains.

The next day we go to Ephesus which is the first of the seven churches listed in the Book of Revelation. Messiah is revealed here as "The One who holds the seven stars in His right hand, the One who walks among the seven golden lampstands." It is an incredible archeological site. Way better than Colossae, people! Remember the pile of dirt? This place is amazing. Remnants of a medical building, office and storefronts, even a public toilet and of course the famous library.

My favorite part of Ephesus, the "loveless church," was not the things left behind that marked that man was here, but the marks that were left behind that showed that believers in the Messiah were here. Let me explain. The "Ichthus" pronounced ikh-thoos is a Greek word simply meaning fish. It is spelled; Iota, Chi, Theta, Upsilon, Sigma. These five Greek letters stand for the meaning, "Jesus Christ, Son of God, Savior." In Greek, "Lesous Christos, Theou Uios, Soter." This symbol was used by the early believers as a means of identifying or acknowledging another believer. Remember, Christian's were persecuted by Rome.

Our guide in Turkey bends down and picks up a piece of chalk. He then points out a circle carved into the stone and begins to show us the meaning of what looks like a "game board." He reveals how this circle or wheel with six spokes making six wedges is really the Greek Ichthus lettering. Using the chalk he draws down the middle and makes the Iota (looks like the letter I), then the Chi (looks like an X), the Theta is the circle itself (letter

O), the Upsilon (Y-shaped), and lastly the Sigma (bent E-shape). Remember, how Naphtali told us about a "game" played on the streets of Jerusalem when Christ was arrested. Well, these are the same markings! This is not a game, people! It's Jesus! I can't draw this out in the book because the formatting is limited but if you go to my website listed in the back of the book, I have the actual video of our guide making the marks of Jesus in Ephesus! This church may be famous for being "loveless," but I love this, people!

We went on to visit the Museum of Ephesus, Carpitium where we learned about making carpets, the Temple of Artemis, and the Church of St. John where it is thought that John the Apostle is buried. The next day we go to Priene, Miletus, the Temple of Apollo, and Kusadasi.

Patmos is our first stop the next day. This is the place that John wrote the Book of Revelation in a cave. Crete is where we visit a Minoan palace; Santorini is the next stop before going on to Corinth. After Corinth, we go to Athens. While others in our group climb the Acropolis and tour the Parthenon, I discover Mars Hill. It's not where they pointed to before, people! I spent a long time up there alone and praying. God is so good! He does give you the desires of your heart! Sometimes you just have to wait!

I leave out from Athens on July 6th. I started this journey on June 14th. I cannot wait to get home to my family of three. I came home realizing that this was the last time I would travel single. I am ready for a change!

Looking back, Joe and I spent the rest of July, August, and September removing "Cat" from his home. We replaced carpets with hardwood floors and got rid of soft furniture. We painted every inch of the home. This home no longer looked like the old home. We worked in the yard too. I was covered in poison ivy! While I was gone, Joe made a circle out of flat stones in the back yard where we will have our wedding ceremony. I think he missed me too!

My mother used to say that I could not get married until I was forty-two. I was forty-two when I agreed to marry Joe. Does that count?

I decided not to type out all of chapter two and three from the Book of Revelation, but I encourage you to go there and to read them. It will be a blessing! No really, it says, you will be blessed when you read Revelation!

He who has an ear, let him hear what the Spirit says to the churches.

Revelation 3:22 (NASB)

Ugh! Pigs Do Fly!

I have been waiting, a whole book, to write this chapter! I wonder if God says, that about us! He has been waiting our lifetime, to put His mark on us showing everyone that we belong to Him! It is about three weeks before the wedding, and we have finally pulled the house together enough to stop the work on the house and get to work on the wedding. I have done nothing for the wedding except mail out email invites. The rest just sort of took on a life of its own. Our desire for our wedding was to have all four of our kids here with their spouses and the grandbabies. Yes, I will be a grandmother to two most wonderful kids. I am just a little excited! We are having a small wedding in the backyard with cake and cold drinks, family, and a few friends.

I wake up on a Monday morning and tell my college bound child that today is the day to go and get a dress. We go after her classes finish. We walk in, and a very nice lady helps us. "What kind of dress do you want?" she asks. "I don't know." "Well, let's do it this way. "What don't you want?" I go into a large list of no bling, feathers, tulle, puffy, shiny, outrageous, etc. Simple. She grins and brings me three. She says, "The first one is the one you want, but I brought the other two to give you options. Smart woman! I try on the first dress and love it. It's simple and has a soft fabric with a nice gentle flower pattern. I try on the other two but come right back to this one. This is it. That was easy! She asks, "When is the wedding? Three weeks. It seems God has good timing; today is the last possible day to buy a dress and get it altered in enough time to have it for the wedding. I need inches off the bottom. I am short, people! She asks about the style of wedding and if I have shoes. "Nope." She brings me a low pair of cute sandals. Perfect! She's good!

There is no family of the bride with a wedding budget. But Father God shows up and provides again. Every couple of days for the next couple of days fun things happen. I get a thought of "square bowls." Wait, what? I am driving, and God says to pull over and go into "Target." No, not *that "Target,"* the store Target. I go in and come out clueless. *What Lord? I missed it.* But then I look over and see the party store. I had been in there before and found nothing. I decide to go in and I find the large plastic trays that I need for the cakes and the square bowls. I even find large plastic dimes and two plastic pigs. I plan to glue wings on them and crash them into the wedding cake.

Then one day we decide on a color theme. My favorite flower is a rose that is orange and yellow that blends and have red tip edges. "Joseph's Coat" is the name of the rose. Aalia's dress is her prom dress that a nice lady does a great job shortening and making it fit perfectly. It's a pretty blend of green into yellow. Aalia and I decide to use the nice green, lemon yellow, and orange as the wedding colors. Not your typical colors, but seriously, after three books, really, people! I had another one of those obedience moments, and I pull into a store parking lot. I go in and look around. The ribbons are marked more than fifty-percent off. But get this, only the yellow, orange, and exact color green ones. Oh and one other one. A white one that says, "Happily Ever After." So I pass them up. No, seriously, I buy them. I am just messing with you. I am getting tired. I've written three books in less than eight months! I'm getting giddy, people! It's almost done!

Our plan was simple, right? The house to serve the food, the backyard to have the ceremony. I would make the cakes. Mr. Richard would do the ceremony. I will fix the flowers myself. We would do a little bit of decorating. Well, it seems that the word got around, and people started asking if they could come to the wedding. Part of me started thinking this is not a freak show, and then I started thinking, maybe they don't think that I will go through with it, and they want to be there when I bolt. Either way, the guest list grows. We have to rent more chairs.

It's Saturday, one week before the wedding. We have moved the stairs from the back porch to the other side. This means that there is a hole in front of the deck that needs dirt. We plan to get dirt this morning to fill in the hole before next week. Aalia goes to take Adam to baseball practice, and she takes the truck. She has a truck accident and totals the car she hits. She is ok, and so is our truck (PTL for steel bumpers!). The dirt store is closed. We buy lots of bags of dirt at another store and fill in the hole. We have another problem. We have had another rough, dry summer, and the backyard doesn't look good.

Just a couple of days before the wedding now. We have moved all of our stuff out of the apartment and cleaned it up to turn over to the property manager by the ninth. Whatever stuff that was left in the apartment is now in the garage. We are officially at the house now with me sleeping in Aalia's room for a couple of days. It looks like a battle zone.

In comes the daughter and son-in-law from Florida. Adam and Aalia are playing nerf guns with the grandkids. I pick one up and come around the corner to shoot at my future grandson. I shoot Joe's son in the head. Yup, smack in the middle of the forehead. Oh, did I mention that I had not officially met him yet? Nice to meet you! Great first impression, literally a dent in the head. Paula and Greg arrive. I am marrying Joe so that Paula will be my sister. I still tell him that.

We spend the day having everyone helping around the house. We spread out pine needles all over the backyard to hide the dead grass and set up white chairs for the now two hundred guests that say they are coming. Joe and I want to set up a small pond with a fountain near the rock circle. It should take only a couple of hours! My famous last words. I bake the wedding cakes and do the base coats of frosting. Grocery shopping gets done, and the flowers arrive. I plan to do those myself as well. The gang is getting hungry, and Greg takes Aalia with him, and they go and pick up pizzas from the pizza place. They come home with ten pizzas. It figures. Everyone is tired at the end of the day. They are staying at a nearby hotel. We all go to bed tired. Joe sleeps in the bedroom with all of the cakes on small tables. He is in cake heaven.

The day before the wedding is a Saturday. A local gas station has put up a sign that says:

"Big Day! 10-10-10, my dimedeal.com" I almost crashed my truck when I saw it.

I've got three crockpots cooking taco soup to serve at the rehearsal dinner, and I am still cooking and frosting. The flowers are iced until the morning, and we try to pull together enough to rehearse the wedding. Mr. Richard seems nervous. I keep reminding him that it will be his fault if something goes wrong. No pressure! It's hot for October! I wear a t-shirt that says, "I believe in flying pigs" as Adam practices walking me down the aisle. Everyone is watching. I get down to the rock circle and Adam hands me off to Joe with a pat on Joe's shoulder and comments, "She's your problem now." I guess everyone was listening too because they are all laughing.

Mr. Richard has gone over our vows with us so many times that Joe and I have memorized them. Mr. Richard has done a wonderful job and written out the meaning of covenant, and the ceremony is beautiful. But Joe and I are tired and getting silly. We mimic the vows and crack each other up. Mr. Richard keeps giving us "the look." But with one more really funny one, I say, "High four and a half" and Joe and I clap our hands together. Joe's son realizes what we have just done and hangs his head in shame. So that you know Joe has a permanently bent pinky finger on one of his hands. I told him I would marry him when he got his "act" straight. Well, that never happened, and instead, we replaced high fives with high four and a half's.

My sweet friends Amy, Stephanie, and Requelle are singing and John the musician is playing. I am walking down the aisle to "Come Thou Fount." My sweet friend, Requelle, suggests we do it again, the walking down part because I came down the aisle at "Prone to wander Lord I feel it." Wait, what? I don't have a problem with that! It's just who I am, people!

The evening is just a mess of friends and family, oh yeah, and Mr. Richard. We eat taco soup and brownies and have a good time getting to know one another. Tomorrow is the big day. Everyone leaves all at once. Joe and I look at each other. Boy, do we have some work to do. In comes Amy, Stephanie, and Requelle to save the day. Did I tell you how great my friends are? Well, Stephanie and Requelle go off to the garage with Aalia. Stephanie decorates the granddaughter's flower basket and Requelle and Aalia make a ribbon decoration by gluing ribbon onto a trim board for behind the cakes. All three of them make ribbon ties to hang in the trees tomorrow.

Amy stays in the kitchen with me cooking. We need something from the store, so Joe volunteers. While he is gone, Amy and I talk about how God worked to bring Joe in my life. It is not a magic formula, and it is not something that I "did" or was even looking for. It is God's timing, and I help her with some plans of her own. It's good to encourage one another on toward love and good deeds. I read that in a really good book! Look up Hebrews 10: 24!

Joe comes back in. It's late, and he is really tired. He had also hit Amy's car when he backed out of the driveway. Amy handles it like a true friend. Don't worry; we will settle it after the honeymoon. So that you know, this car is her baby. We hit her baby, and she is staying late and washing our dishes! Ugh!

The day has arrived. It's October 10, 2010. Yes, this is the day pigs fly. I have said this for so long, and now I am having way too much fun with this. I have made a piñata shaped like a flying pig, and it will hang in the trees above the circle of rocks where we will get married. I'm hoping people crack up when they notice it. When you come up to the house, there is a small basket full of pink flying pigs that the kids can play with and launch anytime they like. I also have mums everywhere and big plastic dimes. The fountain works, and there are petals and dimes floating in the water. It only took a couple of hours to make, people! Ok, I confess. It took way longer than that. There are ribbons hanging in the trees, and I have just decorated the wedding cake with Joseph's coat roses and flower petals and a dime on top of the cake. Time to crash the pigs into the side of the cake. That is my favorite part.

I am still working on the flowers and realize that I have less than an hour to shower and get ready. I get some folks to help with the food and go off to shower. I shower and hear guests arriving. I get out of the shower and start to dry my hair. I still have long black thick hair and what was I thinking! It takes forever to dry! I flip my hair down and start to blow dry from the roots. Bad idea, I never do this. Now I smell smoke and hear horrible noises. Sparks fly, and I quickly unplug the hair dryer.

I am wet, naked, and stuck upside-down with my hair caught in the hair dryer. The smoke is my hair burning, and I am naked! I crack the door open and call for help. No one. Two hundred guests and not a bugger in the place to help. I see my phone and call Aalia. Praise the Lord that my kid never puts her phone down. She comes to her mother's rescue. Since I have killed the hairdryer, she goes off to get her straightener. I put on some clothes. She straightens my hair as I get dressed and put makeup on. I will not be wearing a veil or scarf. I have issues, people!

I hear the music start. Stop the music! Stop the music! I'm not ready yet! My heart wanted to yell that with everything in me. But the Lord stepped in, in His most wonderful loving and kind way He says, "You will never admit to being ready to get married baby girl. You will never think that you are ready." With that, I just had to laugh and breathe and cry some tears. A quick picture with Adam and Aalia and I head to the dining room to go out the door.

My new grandson Kaleb is walking down the aisle carrying our rings. I have not told you about our rings. Early on I told Joe that I did not want any other ring for my wedding band. I had my "Yeshua" ring from Israel, and I wanted to use that. God gave me a hug when He gave me that ring. Joe took my Yeshua ring into a jeweler. He had his wedding ring and the wedding ring of his wife melted down and made into one ring. The jeweler said that he could copy the design and wrote "Yeshua" in Hebrew on Joe's wedding band. God gave Joe a hug when He gave him that ring. God is in the details, people! Don't forget to slow down and look!

My cousin helps me get my shoes on. I look at the box that they came from. The name of the shoe is "Kyra." I tear up because that is a unique name and it belongs to my granddaughter who is heading up the aisle throwing flower petals and looking adorable with her pretty dress and her gorgeous curly hair. Adam has my arm, and they open the back door. I step out right on cue, sorry Requelle, I step out to "Prone to wander Lord I feel it" and it all just seems right. Adam walks me up the aisle behind Aalia. He hands me off to Joe, pats him on the shoulder and comments, "Good luck." The guests all laugh, and Mr. Richard begins.

He talks about the covenant of marriage, and this will be my covenant marriage. I can't help but be overwhelmed by God. I am usually not this mushy. I keep tearing up, and when it comes to me saying my vows, I have trouble talking. Yup, I know what you are thinking! Miracles, people! But at one point I tear up, and Joe gets out his handkerchief and dries my eyes. How much does God love me? In the words of Adam when he was younger, "Bigger than enough." How much does God love me? In the gentleness of Joe Nahler, "Bigger than enough."

We break with tradition and don't do the "kiss the bride part." Oh, I can't kiss in public, people! Serious, three books and you have not figured out my issues? We really want to do the Lord's Supper. Our four children and their spouses pass around the bread and the grape juice. A quicky kiss behind my flower bouquet and we are man and wife. Aalia has a funny song play as we come down the aisle, and people throw petals on us. That is a blessing you know!

We eat and laugh. We talk with dear friends and enjoy our afternoon. We also sweat! It is October, but it feels like July! I was in "bride-mode" and Mr. Richard almost left the wedding without signing the paperwork. Thank you, God, for Terri, his wife who reminded him! Our hearts are full! While talking to our guests, we keep hearing everyone talk about a bird that kept singing so loudly over us during the ceremony. Wait, what bird? It isn't until later when we replay the video that you hear this beautiful bird singing the entire time during our ceremony. Joe and I did not hear it. We both felt like we were in a private protective bubble, in front of two hundred people! But we never heard it. I'm so thankful that friends were able to video the service so we can remember all that the Lord has done! He really did sing over me, and Joe, and it was not something that man "made" happen. It was all God and His little bird. God is so incredibly good!

I spent most of my singleness spinning around in circles shouting "la la la la" or "when pigs fly" at the very mention of marriage. I always figured that if God were to introduce someone into my life, He would have to set Joe directly in front of me, slap me upside the head. God used a hairdryer. And He would have to proceed to tell me that Joe is the one for me. I have flying pigs in my wedding cake, people! I also figured that, when I introduced this new guy to Mr. Bob, Miss Tammy, Hailey, Logan, Landon, and Mr. Richard, if they did not like him or if he did not fit in well, it would be the door for him! Well, he fits right in, and I got my Ruth socks blown off!

Looking back, I really didn't think that I would ever get here. And by that here, I mean both at a place to get remarried and at a place where this trilogy of books is coming to an end. God really does want a relationship with each and every one of us. My whole reason to write all of this down was not to celebrate me but to celebrate The One Who made me. I am excited about what Jesus has done in my life!

The LORD your God is in your midst, a victorious warrior. He will exult over you with joy, he will be quiet in His love, He will rejoice over you with shouts of joy (singing).

Zephaniah 3:17 (NASB)

"For your husband is your Maker, whose name is the LORD of Hosts; and your Redeemer is the Holy One of Israel, who is called the God of all the earth. For the LORD has called you, like a wife forsaken and grieved in spirit, even like a wife of one's youth when she is rejected," says your God. "For a brief moment I forsook you, but with great compassion, I will gather you. In an outburst of anger I hid My face from you for a moment, but with everlasting lovingkindness, I will have compassion on you," says the LORD your Redeemer.

Isaiah 54:5-8

Invitation

In the Book of Mark, the leper that comes to Jesus and is healed by Jesus is also excited about Jesus.

And a leper came to Jesus, beseeching Him and falling on his knees before Him, and saying, "If You are willing, You can make me clean."

Mark 4:40 (NASB)

Lepers had a contagious type of skin disorder. But there is a spiritual condition identified with leprosy in the Scriptures. Leprosy shows up on individuals relating to pride-fullness. King Uzziah was from the Tribe of Judah but went into the Temple area that only those from the Tribe of Levi could go. He went inside in pride and came out covered in leprosy. Miriam, the sister of Moses, spoke in pride and got leprosy. Even Moses put his hand in his garment and brought it out covered in leprosy and put it back and brought it out clean again. The rabbinical teachers believed that leprosy came from God, and only God could heal it.

So this man comes to Jesus as a leper (pride), but he comes to Him praying and in a humbled positioning. He asks for healing, but the way that he asks means that if it is Jesus' desire to heal him, then he will be healed. But this man who has been humbled will still believe in Jesus even if he is not healed.

Moved with compassion, Jesus stretched out His hand and touched him, and said to him, "I am willing; be cleansed."

Mark 4:41 (NASB)

Jesus is moved by the man's positioning and touches the man. Now only Jesus, God With Us, can touch a man with a contagious skin disorder with no fear of getting it Himself. He touches the leper with authority and power, and by saying the man is clean. He is revealing Himself as God With Us, Emmanuel.

Immediately the leprosy left him and he was changed.

Mark 4:42 (NASB)

The leper is healed, but of course, Jesus is Emmanuel! The man has had an intimate touch from God, and the man is changed!

And He sternly warned him and immediately sent him away, and He said to him, "See that you say nothing to anyone; but go show yourself to the priest and offer for your cleansing what Moses commanded, as a testimony to them."

Mark 4:43-44 (NASB)

Jesus commands the man with authority and casts him away saying tell no one what He has done but go and fulfill the Law of Moses. Jesus came to fulfill the law and not to change it or get rid of it.

But he went out and began to proclaim it freely and to spread the news around to such an extent that Jesus could no longer publicly enter a city, but stayed out in unpopulated areas; and they were coming to Him from everywhere.

Mark 4:45 (NASB)

But this man who has been healed, and who has been changed, is so excited that he tells everyone! He writes it down for generations to see what Jesus has done. He shares it with everyone he knows, come, see what God has done for me! Little old me! Because of the man's testimony of what God has done, Jesus can only teach out in the wilderness, the place to depend on God, because He can no longer publically enter a city.

I want to be like that healed and changed man! I wrote these three books, not to tell of what I have done because basically, I have been stubborn, disobedient, whinny, careless, sleepy, naked, poor, blind, and pitiful. Sounds like a sick and wrong set of princess dwarfs!

I wrote this down because I identify with the former leprous man. I have been healed! I have been changed! I have been set free! I have been saved! No more veils for me, people!

I plan to share the Good News of the Gospel of Jesus Christ with everyone that I meet. This starts with you!

Do you have a personal relationship with the Most High God?

First, admit to God that you are a sinner.

It's ok, we all are sinners. We all have to admit this. The Bible says, "For all have sinned and fall short of the glory of God." Romans 3:23

Second, ask God to forgive you for your sins.

Sin leads to death. We have to repent or turn away from our old ways and turn to God and His ways. The Bible says, "For the wages of sin is death, but the gift of God is eternal life in Christ Jesus our Lord." Romans 6:23

Third, believe in Jesus and that you must be born again.

Jesus says, "I am the way and the truth and the life. No one comes to the Father except through Me." John 14:6. He also said, "I tell you the truth, unless a man is born again, he cannot see the kingdom of God." John 3:3

Fourth, believe in your heart that Jesus Christ died on the cross for you and that He rose again.

When Jesus died on the cross and rose again from the dead, He made a way for sinful-unholy man to live forever with a sinless-Holy God. Romans 10:9-11 says it beautifully, "That if you confess with your mouth, 'Jesus is Lord,' and believe in your heart that God raised Him from the dead, you will be saved. For it is with your heart that you believe and are justified, and it is with your mouth that you confess and are saved. As the Scripture says, 'Anyone who trusts in Him will never be put to shame.'"

Fifth, you need to surrender your life to Jesus and ask Him to be both your Lord and your Savior.

This is the part where you invite Him to come into your life and into your heart. Asking Him to be your Savior means that you recognize that you are a sinner, and your sins have a price that needs to be accounted for. The cost of sin or the ultimate price to be paid for sin is death. Jesus paid the ultimate price for your sins by paying for them on the cross. He died for you. Your debt has been paid, and you stand clean, free of debt in front of God, sinless because of Jesus. He saved you from your sins thus He is your Savior. Asking Him to be your Lord means that you are asking Him to become Master and Teacher of your life. Where He leads, you will follow. What He teaches, you will learn. You are asking Him to be in a relationship with you.

If you want you can pray using your own words or pray a prayer like this:

God, I have sinned against you. I want you to forgive me for all of my sins. I believe that Jesus died on the cross for me and that He rose again. I want to surrender my life to You God. You can use me as you wish. I want Jesus to come into my life and into my heart to be my Lord and my Savior. I ask this in Jesus' name. Amen

Why do you pray in Jesus' Name? Because not only is there power in the Name of Jesus but by defining who's name you pray in means that you define to Whom you belong. For me, it is easy. I belong to Jesus, and I will joyfully pray in His Name!

Why do we say, "Amen." Because Amen means verily, verily or truly, truly. What I have just prayed I truly believe, and I verify, meaning demonstrate that I believe my words to be true and accurate.

It's really simple, but it will change your life, and you will celebrate forever.

Jesus has made a way for us to accept Him as our Lord and Savior by dying on the cross for us. When we accept Him into our hearts and lives, we allow Him to change us from "impure/unholy" to "pure/holy." He makes a way for us to live out eternity with a Holy God. It's a really good plan, people!

Please don't miss your opportunity to be touched and made "clean" by Jesus! It is the best, most refreshing, and peaceful thing you can do in your life. It will change your life. Jesus will change your life!

Then after you do, we can go around and tell everyone in the town and anyone who is willing to hear about what God has done for both of us! You can admit publically that you are a child of the Most High God and part of God's family! Hopefully, your testimony will fill up the buildings and Bible studies with people who want more of Him in their lives too!

God is so good! He really is!

Epilogue

I want to thank you for taking the time to read the first three books that I have written which are the testimony of my life up to my wedding on October 10th, 2010.

I thought that it would be fun to share just a few updates with my readers since I wrote the books in 2016.

- Amy was wonderful, and we got the insurance worked out, and her car is fixed. She is also now married! God is so good!
- We had so much food from the wedding that we fed the Bible studies for a week! Fishes and loaves! God is so good!
- We returned from Hawaii and Rabbi Baruch was in town. We took our Ketubah (wedding contract) to him, and he signed it along with two others who were at the wedding, Craig and Richard H. God is so good! And Joe is stuck with me!
- My home church did break into two pieces. But God is good. We all learned a lot about ourselves and our personal walks with the Lord. No comfort zones, people! God is so good!
- Adam graduated from his private Christian school in 2012. Another promise of God fulfilled! God is so good!
- I still drive the Chevy S-10! It has over two hundred thousand miles on it. It is just missing some front teeth thanks to Aalia's accident before the wedding. This truck is the energizer bunny! God is so good!
- Joe and I went to Israel and Jordan in 2012. It was a wonderful trip full of great adventures, but one of the best parts was the security. Just as the usual pull me out of line part happens, they ask, "Who are you traveling with?" I say, "My husband." They motion him forward and take a look at his paperwork and wave us through. I got to go through the regular turnstiles! Like normal, people! Have white guy, will travel!

- Joe and I got to renew our vows in that little church in Cana. And we got to be baptized together in the Jordan River! God is so good!
- As we crossed over from Israel to Jordan, several of us on the bus were taking pictures, but they only made me get off of the bus. They asked for my passport. The border guard thought that she scored a home run. After questioning, they made me erase my camera memory card. I would have lost my whole trip. EXCEPT that the night before the Lord led me to change my memory card and put it away. I put in a brand new one. I only lost less than a hundred pictures. God is so good.
- I found out later also through Facebook that a childhood friend of mine from Afghanistan has also become a believer in Christ Jesus. I was scared to talk to him, so I contacted his sweet wife Susan first. But on Facebook, it said that his favorite book was the Holy Bible. I prayed and sent them my phone number. I got the greatest call back from Farhad! What an absolute joy to have a brother and sister in Christ Jesus! God is so good! Pray for their family to know Christ too!
- Aalia graduated college in 2014. God is so good!
- Joe and I felt the Lord's leading and we moved to a new home that fits us perfectly. We call it our "place of peace." I once told Joe when I saw a house in the woods that belonged to a famous author, "I could write books too if I lived in a house in the woods." God is so good!
- My sweet Joe has had cancer surgeries and an almost fatal tick bite, and we are beyond thankful to the Lord for healing. God is so good!
- Adam is starting back to college this fall, and he will be completing a double major. God is so good!
- I have been laid off, again. Seriously, I have! This time from Lifelines. God told me it was coming. The funding for the ministry was down, and I knew it was ending a season. I still volunteer and do Mr. Richard's newsletter and office work for him. It is easier than trying to teach him how to do it. So I guess I kind of still work for him, only for free. Because of being laid off I have been able to devote almost

eight months to finally getting my testimony written down. God is so good!

- I now have four grandbabies! My Jacob calls me "Nana Sha-key." I love it and won't let anyone tell him otherwise. Baby Micah is only a few months old, but he has already stolen his Nana's heart. I thank Joe every day for making me a Nana. God is so good!
- I now have two nephews and a niece! Please continue to pray for my brother and his sweet family! God is so good!
- Because of writing my testimony, I have a family member I never knew existed. What a blessing! God is so good!
- My dad and I have an off and on relationship. We have gone years without any communication. I have no explanations. But God is good even when questions go unanswered!
- Joe doesn't drink alcohol at all. No wine! Joe is my partner in dimes! What a gift from God, he is! God is so good!
- I had lots of friends that were concerned about our age difference. I was too at first. Joe's is older than Mr. Richard. That's like older than dirt times two! But we both have a great sense of humor about it and God has knit us into one with Him. That either makes Joe a forty-nine-year-old woman or me a sixty-nine-year old-man. Either way, it works! God is so good!
- I have stayed married for six years! Longer than the first time, people! God is so good!
- I get asked to speak and share my faith in small groups and area churches. One of the questions that I get asked the most is, "How do you witness to Muslims?" Well, there is no secret formula or magic set of steps. Be real in your own relationship with Christ, share Jesus with them, and get them a Bible in their language. Only Jesus can change a heart! But be there for them when they ask questions and give them Biblical answers, not opinions.
- I just read this to Joe, and he is laughing at me because I called it a "Prelude" instead of an "Epilogue." It's just details, people. Maybe this means it's the end of the trilogy but the beginning of other books! God is still good!

Books By Shahe Nahler

Volume One

Born Afghan, Born American, Born Again

This is my testimony of leaving Islam, becoming a Christian, and living a new life in Jesus.

Volume Two

Born Muslim, Became Christian, Beloved Israel

This is my story of letting go of Islam, living out my Christianity, and loving my Jewish Jesus.

Volume Three

My Journey, My Jesus, My Joe

This is my story of being the beloved of God, falling in love with Jesus, and marrying my husband, Joe.

If you would like more information or have questions, please feel free to contact me at

www.shahesart.com

www.shahenahler.wordpress.com

Thanks for reading my books! Shahe

Made in the USA
Columbia, SC
08 October 2017